Scraps From
My Sabretasche

Scraps From My Sabretasche

The Experiences of a Trooper of the
14th Light Dragoons in India
& During the Indian Mutiny

L E Warner

&

George Carter Stent

LEONAUR

Scraps From My Sabretasche
The Experiences of a Trooper of the
14th Light Dragoons in India
& During the Indian Mutiny

by L E Warner

&

George Carter Stent

First published under the title
Scraps From My Sabretasche

Leonaur is an imprint
of Oakpast Ltd

ISBN: 978-0-85706-176-8 (hardcover)
ISBN: 978-0-85706-175-1(softcover)

http://www.leonaur.com

Publisher's Notes

In the interests of authenticity, the spellings, grammar and place names
used have been retained from the original editions.

The opinions of the authors represent a view of events in which he
was a participant related from his own perspective,
as such the text is relevant as an historical document.

The views expressed in this book are not necessarily
those of the publisher.

Contents

CHAPTER 1

Canterbury

And especially, from every shire's end
Of Englelond, to Canterbury they wende,
The holy blisful martyr for to seke,
That hem hath holpen, when that they were seke.—Chaucer.

Dear old Canterbury! with its castellated gateway, meet entrance into so ancient a city—its quaint narrow streets, pervaded with an air of quietness and repose;—its antiquated, gabled and bow-windowed houses; its hostelries, where even Chaucer's pilgrims may have put up; its alms-houses, with ancient-looking men and women standing in the doorways, suggestive of those who stood there in like manner ages ago;—its remains of convents, monasteries, and castles;—its ramparts and towers, hoary with age, but only enhanced in their massive grandeur, *grand* by their antiquity, mutely telling of the fierce fights they witnessed, of the strong hands that built them, and the stout hearts that defended them a thousand years ago. Its "Dane John" with its historic mount, the pride and boast of the inhabitants, thrown up in one night, and containing in its bosom the bodies of ten thousand Danes killed in battle there, forming at once a tomb and monument more expressive far than the most elaborate structures of stone or marble; and lastly, its glorious cathedral, standing in majestic grandeur in the centre of the City, towering above—far over-topping everything—a visible embodiment of the overmastering principles for the propagation and defence of which it was reared:—

Fine and strong
'T has stood for long,
Jetting up its slender lances
Far athwart the arched sky,
On whose tops the sunshine glances,

While the birds wing brightly by.

For, enter the city which way you will from its beautiful environs, and its tall spires are beheld standing out against the sky, rearing their lofty fanes into the clouds; from every street it seems to look calmly and pityingly down on the puny and fretting cares of the passing generations who have trodden its time-worn stones.

Well may the city be called "ancient." Few places can boast of such, relics of the mighty past as Canterbury, or such historic and legendary associations as are connected with it, coupled with such names as those of Saint Augustine, Chaucer, Edward the Black Prince, Thomas a'Becket, and a host of other celebrities. But, though, the passing stranger, the well-read casual visitor, may enter somewhat into these more general considerations, it is only those whose opening years were passed amid these scenes that can enter into living communion with the green lanes and varied scenery of hill and dale, woods and cornfields, by which it is surrounded. How often have I rambled through the many shady walks, and from Harbledown, St. Thomas's, St. Martin's, or one of the many hills that encircle the city, have looked dreamily at it as it lay nestled in the heart of the valley, with the Stour flowing through its midst.

What excursions to "Park Alley," "Whitehall," "Burntwood," "Fish-Pool Bottom," or other well-known spots, nutting, lilying, or primrosing as the case might be!—But to return within the sacred precincts; for it is around these venerable piles that the vivid memories of my boyhood cling with strongest, even feverish, tenacity. What awe I used to feel if I had occasion to pass one of the old churches at night!—and what a sigh of relief I gave when once out of the influence of their venerated and yet dreaded locality! How we boys, too, used to gloat over the old tales of the "Haunted House" in the cathedral yard, and, numbers giving confidence, though with an involuntary bristling up of the hair at the remembrance of the ghostly legends connected with those places, proceed there in a body, and from thence, whooping and yelling to keep ourselves mutually in countenance, through the cloisters and the "Dark Entry," until chased out of the cathedral precincts by "Old Leather Breeches," the lame guardian of that sacred locality.

I can remember, too, how, when growing older, liking to go into the cathedral, and while the service was going on in the chancel, staying in the aisle listening with rapt attention and delight to the clear melodious voices of the boy choristers, almost fancying at times some heavenly choir must be fluttering overhead, warbling their angelic notes,—or, as the organ pealed forth its diapason, wondering where such sounds could possibly come from;—above, below, everywhere seeming to be loaded with harmony—the whole air impregnated with melody.

> *And the anthem slowly rolls,*
> *Over the assembled souls,*
> *With a free*
> *Full melody.*

Drinking in this delightful music, I would alternately gaze up with admiration to the beautiful stained windows.

> *With softened shine*
> *From every pane*
> *Whose gorgeous stain*
> *Lies upon*
> *The pavement stone,*
> *Telling many an awful story*
> *Of the martyr-days divine;*
> *While a dim torch-lighted glory*
> *Streams from every pictured shrine;*

or the gold and enamelled groined roof,—the whole of which was popularly believed to have been done by a woman, though how she could possibly have got up there, or being there, could have done such masterly workmanship, I could never conceive,—the looking up alone made me feel giddy. But my greatest delight was in wandering from one monument to another, somehow lovingly lingering near those which commemorated soldiers who had fallen in battle.

> *Many warriors here about*
> *Lie, some with crossed hands devout,*

These monuments, with their long lists of officers and men, and the tattered colours drooping over them, were peculiarly attractive to me. The colours, to me, vividly telling their tales of bloody Indian battles, of deadly struggles for those very flags—of their handles having often felt the death-grip not relaxed even in death. Who could tell how many brave men those colours had led on to victory or death? How many eyes had looked on them as their guiding star to glory! How many had reverenced them as pilgrims would some sacred relic! How many had fought, bled, and died to prevent their being tarnished! I used to feel a sort of choking in the throat, almost amounting to a sob, a swelling of the chest, and a humidity about the eyes when I thought of all this, and fancy it was worth fighting and dying for to be thus honoured; that I would gladly brave anything could I but have my name inscribed on one of those lists of heroes, and I would think to myself "Who knows but some day a monument may also be placed here to my memory?" I felt all this then. But this rhapsody about Canterbury and its cathedral[1] can hardly be expected to interest the general reader as it does one who loves every stick and stone of the old place—even the memory of the brave little fellow belonging to the "King's School," who once challenged me out to fight in the "Green Court," and who gave me such a severe thrashing. This love for Canterbury is easily accounted for. *I was born there.*

---

1. While writing the above, I was dismayed by receiving an account of the fire at Canterbury Cathedral; fortunately if was extinguished before any irreparable damage was done.

CHAPTER 2

Maidstone

See those ribbons gaily streaming;
I'm a soldier now, Lisette,
I'm a soldier now, Lisette,
And of battles I am dreaming,
And the honours I shall get.

"If you stick a pint, I'll give you a respectable crop." This expressive sentence was addressed to me by Private Cook, familiarly styled Charley Cook, the individual appointed to cut the hair of all recruits joining the depôt of H. M.'s 14th (King's) Light Dragoons, for that was the title then of the regiment I had honoured by my choice. Having previously been informed of the difference between a "respectable crop" and a "regimental crop," and having had ocular demonstration, moreover, by seeing living specimens in both styles, I was the better able to draw my own conclusions regarding their separate merits, and decide without hesitation as to the particular crop I should patronise.

For the information of those who are unenlightened on these points, I will endeavour to explain them. A "respectable crop" represents the hair closely cut at the back of the head, but with some portion on each side allowed to remain a trifle longer, so as to enable the wearer to display any taste he may possess in arranging it, by curling (if such a thing were possible), twisting, or otherwise disposing of it. A "regimental crop" consists in the whole of the hair being literally mowed off the head of the victim to one uniform length of about half-an-inch, till it resembles a stubble-field, or a scrubbing brush.

Knowing this, I thought it advisable to propitiate the hair-cutter by "sticking a pint," which I did, to his entire satisfaction, and my own particular delectation; for I should not appear, after undergoing the operation, as if I had just returned from a sojourn in the cells. I, there-

11

fore, requested him to cut my hair exactly like his own, he possessing a luxuriant curly head of hair, that was the envy and admiration of every recruit in the depôt. I need not say that, on drawing comparisons afterwards, I was somewhat disappointed.

I was next introduced to the bathroom, soused into a tub of water, and underwent a sanitary process; my civilian's clothes were taken away, and I was inducted into a "hospital suit," consisting of a sort of blue dressing-gown and drawers with nightcap to match,—and slippers. The whole costume at once unique, and suggestive of fevers and every description of disease that "flesh is heir to."

Then came the bitterest trial of all. I abominate physic! From my earliest infancy no power on earth could make me take even a pill unless it was carefully imbedded in the nicest of jam, yet I was compelled to swallow a tumbler of some diabolical nauseous mixture—necessary to complete my thorough purification, I suppose. Aghast as I was at this fresh innovation—disgusted at the idea of having to swallow the filthy draught—seeing the hospital sergeant, who was a bit of a wag, grinning at the grimaces I made, and determined not to let him have all the laugh to himself, I gulped it down in desperation, smacking my lips as if I had just imbibed nectar instead of the atrocious compound, and held out my glass as if anxious for more. Fortunately he thought I had had sufficient, and I rushed out of the surgery "a sadder and a wiser man."

After having suffered all the horrors of "quarantine" in hospital for two or three days till my uniform was made, I emerged from my chrysalis state into all the glory of a fully-equipped "gay young recruit," and was conducted to the barrack-room, where I was installed in a berth, and was immediately surrounded by a crowd of admiring friends, who were obliging enough to sell me—one, a silver-mounted riding-whip—another, a pair of spurs with *bonâ-fide* "shilling rowels." These being described as absolutely necessary to my respectability as a dragoon, I at once purchased, though I discovered shortly afterwards that I had paid slightly through the nose for them.

Then followed a series of different kinds of "setting up" drills, such as "goose-step," "extension motion," "club-drill," &c., till I should be considered fit to appear in public, that is, allowed to go out of barracks. This process generally occupies a month, and in some cases even two or three; for your awkward man must be licked into shape. before he can "parade his figure" in the streets, the "back-stick" often being extensively used, though I am proud to say I never had one on in my life, being at that time as straight as an arrow, and flattering myself I was rather a smart young fellow. As a matter of fact, few could beat me in feats of strength or agility in any of the athletic games got up by the young fellows in the garrison.

I shall not forget the blank look of surprise of a sergeant who had charge of a squad of us at "club-drill "on one occasion, before I had been at drill three days. We were "standing at ease," and he took that opportunity of explaining to us the many advantages to be derived from this kind of drill, winding up by saying: "There, when any of you can do *this* with the club, I shall dismiss you from the squad" (illustrating it by taking both ends of the club in his hands and putting it "straight arm" over his head behind his back). I at once demurely requested him to dismiss me, as I could do it *now*, or with my joined hands only. However, he did *not* dismiss me then, but reported me favourably to the adjutant, and in a day or two I was dismissed and never after had any "club drill."

In the course of two or three weeks, I, with the members of the squad to which I had been promoted, had made such progress in our various drills that it was considered we might be safely trusted outside without danger of getting entangled with our own legs, or tripping ourselves or others up with our spurs;—in fact, we were supposed now to "know how to walk."

We were dismissed with the following injunction:—"Now, from this time you will be allowed to go out of barracks, and don't let me see any of you go slinking along with humps on your backs, but 'throw a chest'[1] and swagger down the street as if you had five pounds in your pocket, and didn't care a damn for anyone—even if you hav'n't got a penny to your name."

> *He who wears a regimental suit*
> *Oft is poor as any raw recruit.*
> *But what of that?*
> *Girls will follow when they hear the drum,*
> *To view the tassel and the waving plume*
> *That deck his hat.*
> *Oh! he will sing, and, when he's not on duty,*
> *Smoke a cigar and flirt with some gay beauty.*

Of course, we did not fail to carry out these instructions to the best of our power, especially when gallantly "trotting out" one of the fair

---

1. Expand your chest.

"Kentish maids," for whom Maidstone is so justly celebrated. I look back to that time with pleasure and regret, for I spent many happy hours there, and my tastes inclining me to rambling about the pleasant neighbourhood rather than frequenting public-houses, I passed most of my spare time in that manner, generally accompanied by some charming little creature to act as guide, who also liked "going out for a walk"; so that, though I was pretty hard worked in barracks, I was not without compensating enjoyments, and these delicious walks I indulged in on every available opportunity.

My berth in the barrack-room was next to that of a married man, who with his wife and child occupied a corner of the room, a very little larger than their own bed, and was screened off at night by curtains, and so loosely, that while lying on my cot I could, if I chose, see them within their curtained space. This sort of system of married persons living in the same room, though much to be deprecated, was a common occurrence then; but I must say the women behaved with the greatest propriety, and the men carefully abstained from using improper language, treating them in every way with the same respect they would their own sisters or mothers,—a circumstance which, I think, reflected much credit on all parties.

This couple were a most strangely assorted pair: the man being above six feet two inches in height, and withal one of the most ferocious looking fellows I ever met with. This, however, was in appearance only, for he was kind to his wife (who looked like a little wax doll, and scarcely reached to his waist), and they lived very happily together.

Through the diplomacy of my mother, who often visited me, and who made private arrangements regarding me,[2] the pair exercised a sort of general supervision over me; in other words, "looked after me," making me as comfortable as possible, at dinner-time supplying me with "tit-bits" from their own table, which I need not say are not included in a soldier's rations. I was thus in a situation rather to be envied by my comrades, in regard to messing arrangements. I considered myself particularly fortunate, for really the woman behaved to me with all the kindness of a mother, and I take this opportunity to tender her, late as it is, my best thanks.

I was also fortunate in successfully passing my examination by the

2. The reader will please bear in mind that I did not enlist out of poverty, but from a desire to see a little of life in foreign countries. I could have been "bought out" at any moment, if I wished it.

school-master in reading, writing, and arithmetic. This exempted me from "going to school," which is considered a great nuisance by most of the scholars, as it materially shortens the little time they have for their own amusements.

In two or three months I was thoroughly master of "foot" and "carbine drill," and had made great advancement in the "sword exercise." During that period also, at intervals, I had occasional "mounts." These "mounts" most of us used to look forward to with pleasure, in spite of "chafing," the inevitable consequence of "bumping drill" on young beginners.

There is a great amount of fun too, watching the inexperienced rider, carefully placed in a proper position before starting, and noting when the horses start off at the last sound of the word :-r-r-o-o-o-t, utterly independent of the riders; how soon they begin to "lose their position," till after a few rounds some of them *will* ride their horses "from nose to croup"; endeavouring to keep their position at first, afterwards frantically trying to "stick on," and eventually made "field marshals" of.[3]

This is had enough, and trying to their dignity as would-be horsemen, but especially when *insult is added to injury*, in the grim irony conveyed by the Rough-rider's bawling out: "Who authorised you to dismount? How dare you dismount your horse without permission? Never do so again without first asking leave!" The fortunate individuals who manage to "keep their seats" indulge in a suppressed titter, little recking that shortly they will probably share a similar fate.

Luckily, recruits, no matter how often they fall off, never seem to hurt themselves; they invariably select a "soft spot" on which to deposit themselves. I remember once seeing a horse gallop off furiously with a recruit, who received a fall that would inevitably have broken the neck of a civilian. The rough-rider, however, was not the least alarmed, but coolly remarked, "Oh, he's all right; he *knows how to fall!*" And sure enough he did; for to my surprise he got up unhurt, shook himself, and mounted again as if nothing had happened.

At length the time began to draw near when the "drafts" from the different depôts were annually sent to join their respective regiments. All leave is, therefore, stopped at this time, under the impression, I believe, that many who had leave to visit their homes for a few days, might be tempted to overstay their time till the drafts had gone, when they would have to wait another year before they could

3. Thrown.

be sent. Here I was again fortunate, through the diplomacy of my mother, who personally applied to the commandant, and succeeded in getting three days' leave for me, on the express condition that she was to see me safe back at the end of that period. The commandant, therefore, ascertaining I bore an excellent character, sent for me, and spoke in such flattering terms of me and to me, that my mother was quite reconciled to the idea of my being a soldier under the command of such a kind-hearted officer. I came back from my visit punctually at the time appointed.

The day at last arrived, long wished for by some, and long dreaded by others, when the men were to be selected who were to join their regiments in India. My regiment was at this time on active service, engaged in the Sikh War, and many of us were anxious to go out and distinguish ourselves—see a little honour and glory in the shape of fighting, and be in time to get a medal or—something else.

Before calling out the names, however, the officer informed us if any man did not wish to go, to say so, and another might go in his place. Out of nearly a hundred selected from my depôt, one only did not wish to go, and the pale face of a woman looking through the barrack railings with a child in her arms, who would be left behind destitute, spoke eloquently as to *his* reason for not wishing to go, and no one ridiculed him as if he were afraid. Another man immediately stepped out and offered himself as a substitute, so the poor woman had her husband for another year.

That evening orders came out that we were to

March away tomorrow,
At the breaking of the day.

The next morning found us—some two hundred and fifty strong, consisting of drafts from the depôts of the 9th Lancers, 3rd and 14th Light Dragoons—on the high road to Chatham, with the band playing "The Girl I left behind me," and other appropriate tunes. I had often seen regiments leaving Canterbury, so I was somewhat prepared for the scenes I saw on every side. Soldiers and civilians, men and women, all huddled together, walking along—marching was out of the question. The whole "line of march "was one series of leave-taking, some of a very sad nature. Mothers, sisters, sweethearts and wives bidding a long farewell to sons, brothers, husbands, or lovers. Poor Poll Brown clinging to the neck of her lover, and sobbing out her "Good-bye, Bill! You *won't* forget to write to me, darling, *will* you?" And Bill's half-blubbering yet emphatic promise that he would *not* forget—that he *would* write—as he tore himself from her encircling arms, seemed to me quite as pathetic as if the leave-taking were more elaborately worded.

The novelty and bustle for the next few days, perhaps, helped to soften the partings of the men; but how many sad hearts went back to Maidstone to brood over their sorrows? How many "Poll Browns" were there who had bid "goodbye" to their Bills—forever? Who knows?

CHAPTER 3

Chinsurah

Having passed through the usual incidents, consequent upon a long voyage, we safely arrived at Calcutta, and the next day were transhipped to a "flat," which conveyed us to Chinsurah, a place some twenty odd miles above Calcutta. Here were splendid barracks, into which we were duly installed, staring at, and admiring everything, totally unsuspicious of the fate that awaited us. Night came, and with it our enemies, for we had no sooner retired to our cots, and were congratulating ourselves on the prospect of a delightful sleep, after having been cramped up in hammocks for so long, when we were startled by a most appalling scream, that seemed to proceed from a woman almost in the very room we were in. Such a frightful sound I had never before heard in my life, it was one prolonged shriek of agony, dying away into a faint wail, as if nature could endure no more, and sank exhausted under some horrible torture.

Every man jumped off his cot in a moment, anticipating some dreadful scene, but the sound had not yet ceased when it was taken up on all sides—above, below, everywhere. The air seemed peopled with countless invisible forms, who filled it with screams in every tone of voice—in every phase of agony! We were horror-struck—the very blood curdled in our veins, and if our hair had a tendency to pointing upwards through being cut short, that tendency became considerably intensified. One old soldier, however, soon allayed our fears with the *naïve* remark, "Them's jackals!"

After this and other satisfactory explanations, we again turned in and slept peaceably till morning, when we had to answer our names at "roll call." I must say, on seeing the men fall in, that I was struck with their disreputable appearance. One would fancy instead of having been in bed and sleeping comfortably all night, the whole of us had been out drinking and fighting. Black eyes, lumpy foreheads, swollen cheeks, red puffy noses and protruding lips formed the great majority—there was scarcely a man that had not some distinguishing mark on his frontispiece. The old soldier before alluded to was equally happy in his remarks on the subject, and disposed of this second visitation as tersely as he had done the former, but in a much more expressive manner, "Blarsted skaters" in this instance being the explanation we received.

When we had been a short time in Chinsurah we were sent for to "see our accounts," and get our "ship's clearance," or pay, that had accumulated during the voyage; but most of us looked rather blank on finding that instead of having anything to receive, a great many were on the debit side. This, to our dismay, was soon accounted for; after calling over such, items as white clothing and necessary outfit required before proceeding on the line of march, the sergeant-major came to one large item of such a sinister nature that it threw a gloom over everyone, and many a young fellow's enthusiasm for honour and glory got slightly damped for some time to come. The last and most unlooked for item in every man's account was "One coffin," Rs. 16.

Now, I contend that to make a person pay for his coffin while yet living is not only unfair in a business point of view, and shows very sharp practice at the hands of the authorities, but it is calculated to have anything but a cheering influence on fresh arrivals in India. In fact I believe many deaths in India might be traced to this source only; for there are persons so morbidly sensitive in their dispositions, that such a circumstance would prey upon their minds, and they would rapidly qualify themselves to become tenants of the coffins they had already paid for—in other words, they would actually worry themselves to death. Whether I am right or wrong, however, in my remarks, I leave it to medical science to discover.

The unpleasant feelings caused by this singular item, in my ease, soon wore away, and I passed the whole of my leisure time very pleasantly rambling about the neighbourhood, every day seeing something novel and strange, and not the least strange was my first "love adventure" as I shall call it. I was walking out one day with a comrade named Williams, but who, happening to be a Welshman, delighted in the *soubriquet* of "Taffy," when we met a well-appointed carriage and pair, with a native coachman and. footmen in livery, and containing two young ladies. We had several times met this carriage with the same occupants, and in common with the whole of the men believed them to be the daughters of a general who lived in a bungalow on the banks of the river a short distance from the barracks.

They were known, therefore, and spoken of by the men as the "General's daughters," and as such looked up to with all the respect due to the beautiful daughters of so exalted a functionary. On the carriage passing us, I happened to be on the side nearest to it, and what was my surprise and delight when one of them with an angelic smile dropped a three-cornered *billet-doux* at my feet! The carriage rolled on with its lovely burden, but there lay the note fresh from her fairy fingers. I hastily snatched it up, tore it open, and eagerly devoured its precious contents. They were as follows:—

Dear Sir,—Be under the third tree of the avenue leading to the church at 9 o'clock this evening, and you will find one who much wishes to see you.
Amelia.

Every word of that note was indelibly imprinted on my mind at the first glance, yet I could not for the life of me avoid reading it over and over again. Was it a dream? No. This note redolent with fragrance was proof positive that it was real. Had not the delicate tracery of those dear words been formed by her own hand? She loved me! Yes! She, the daughter of a general, loved me, a private soldier! Boldly overturning all the barriers of rank, fortune, and social position, she had dared to tell me so! For was not the note I held in my hand a confession of love? Would she wish to meet me—would she condescend to write to me at all, if she did not love me? I should see her tonight—tell her in the most impassioned language, and with all the eloquence at my command, how dearly I loved her, how I appreciated her devotion in descending from her lofty sphere and deigning to love one so humble as myself.

Ah, would that my heart had some mode of conveying.
Its language in eloquent tones to her ear;
Or could teach to my lips the power of pourtraying,
The love that it feels, true, devoted, sincere.

I should tell her that, though but a common soldier, I would show by my actions that I was made of nobler stuff—that I would strive to make myself worthy of her—that I—"Well, what does it say?" broke in the voice of Taffy, bringing me back from the blissful realms of imagination, for I had been standing "mooning" in the road till his unwelcome voice recalled me back to myself.

"What's it about? Don't keep it *all* to yourself!" exclaimed he. In answer, I read the contents of the note over to him, and he was as much surprised as myself, but somewhat damaged my aerial structures by hinting that perhaps the note was intended for him. What audacity! She love *him*! Of course, I resolutely combated such an absurd idea, but consented that he should accompany me at 9 o'clock to the meeting-place, and I even promised to exert my influence in interesting the sister to bestow her regards on him. This I conceived to be sufficiently magnanimous for any purpose.

The day seemed interminably long, but the longest day generally *will* come to an end, and so it did in this case. Long before 9 o'clock Taffy and myself had posted ourselves under No. 3 tree, and were straining our eyes in every direction. Could a passenger have seen us he would have given us a wide berth, fancying our designs anything but amorous or peaceful. Nine o'clock struck. Every moment I expected to see her form emerge from the darkness, but no form appeared. Still I did not despair, some trifling thing had delayed her; the general had detained her somewhat longer than usual to sing a favourite song, or to play some new piece of music. A thousand things might have happened to cause the delay. The "first post" sounded half-past nine, still no one came. It was time to be getting towards the barracks if we did not wish to be reported absent. Taffy began to get fidgety and suggested a hoax. I repudiated hoaxes altogether. "Do persons of rank and beauty perpetrate hoaxes?" "Not very likely." "Would *she* indulge in a vulgar hoax, and with *me*!" "Impossible."

"Perhaps it's a plot to get us murdered," said Taffy. I felt the note in my pocket, and smiled contemptuously; being dark I suppose he did not observe it, or probably it had no effect on him, for after a pause he whispered, "Well, I shan't stop here any longer. I don't half like this billet, so I shall be off." I felt almost glad that he was going; for one does not like one's hopes and aspirations to be damped by throwing the cold water of doubt and scepticism over them. I was determined to stop at any risk, and till no matter what hour. This I told him, and requested him to "answer for me at watch-setting." He undertook to do so, I, in return, promising to let him know all the particulars of my adventure when I saw him in the morning.

Off went Taffy, and I was "left alone in my glory," buoyed up for some time by the hope that she would yet come, but gradually despairing of seeing her, that night at least, especially when I heard the "last post" sounded. I had never before noticed the peculiar beauty of this sound, but standing alone under the tree, with the rippling waters of the river running gurgling past me, the notes of the trumpets, as they came wafted towards me through the night air, sounded so exquisitely soft and mellow, and seemed so musically yet plaintively to say, "Come home! come home!" that, for a moment, I almost wished I had gone back with Taffy and was safe in barracks; but the very thought was cowardly and I discarded it as unworthy of me; besides, I still clung to the hope that she would yet come.

The last faint notes of the trumpets had scarcely died away in whispering echoes on the opposite bank of the river, when I fancied I heard a movement in the water, as if something or someone was stealthily approaching the shore where I was. I listened attentively—there was evidently something cautiously making its way through the water, and towards me too. Presently I perceived a dark object crawling up the slimy bank. Was it an alligator? It drew nearer. I held my breath, and strained my eyes to make out what it was. It rose up from its crouching position, and an Indian's voice said, "*Bíbí mángte, sahib?*" (Do you want the lady, sir?).

What a load was taken off my breast, and how relieved and delighted I felt at hearing those three words in a strange language, of which I understood but one,—but that one, to me, embodying the whole of the Hindustani language,—*Bíbí* (lady). This Indian then was the messenger who was to lead me to her presence. "*Bíbí?* Yes! Where is she?" I exclaimed.

The Indian responded to my inquiries by pointing out riverwards. I concluded by this that he was instructed to take me to the back of the bungalow which, as I mentioned before, was on the bank of the river; but I would have gone if it had been on the banks of the "bottomless pit" with equal readiness. On inquiring how I was to get there, he made signs for me to mount on his back and he would carry me. Without hesitation I climbed on his back, and he waded slowly out into the dark river, with me clinging to him with all the tenacity of Sindbad's "Old man of the sea," till he came to a "*budgerow*" that was moored some distance from the bank, but which I had not hitherto seen owing to the darkness of the night. The Indian at once carefully deposited me on the deck of this *budgerow*. I had scarcely touched the deck when my ears were assailed by the savage barking of a dog;—someone within seemed to check it, and a soft voice cried "Come in, don't be afraid!"

Afraid! after hearing that musical voice! I entered. There sat the

"General's daughter," looking more beautiful than ever—more lovely even than when she dropped the precious *billet-doux* at my feet; but there too, chained up to the sofa on which she was sitting, was a most ferocious *bull-dog*, glaring at me with his bloodshot eyes, barking fearfully, and making frantic attempts to break his chain and get at me. I was about to move towards her in spite of the fearful proximity of the dog, when she cried out to me to take care, and turning her fair form to the savage monster, she exclaimed, "Down ye divil, or I'll knock the liver out ov ye!"

I was horror-struck for the moment. That one sentence, delivered in such a palpable brogue, descended with sledge-hammer force on my aerial-built castles, and demolished them in a-twinkling, or as she would have expressed it "knocked 'em all to smithereens." To cut the matter short, I soon discovered by her conversation that she was *not* the general's daughter. The ladies had mistaken Taffy and myself for two young officers, the white uniform of privates in the cavalry being almost the same as that of the officers. We, in turn, had mistaken them for *bonâ-fide* ladies, so that the mistake was mutual. However, I left the good lady of the *budgerow* labouring under the pleasant hallucination that I was a cavalry officer, and a probable pigeon to be plucked at her leisure; but I need not say I did not enlighten her as to my romantic ideas concerning her, when I imagined her to be the "general's daughter."

CHAPTER 4

The March

Our march up country was quite a pleasure-trip, and positively enjoyable. It was a *real* march, too, for most of us had the prospect of footing it—railways not being yet in existence in India—to distances varying from 1,000 to nearly 2,000 miles before we reached our respective destinations.

We mustered altogether—cavalry and infantry—somewhere about 1,400 men, and merrily we used to trudge over the road, lightly equipped, for we carried no arms or appointments; light in pocket, for care had been taken that we should not have a superfluity of cash; and light-hearted, for we were young and hopeful. The monotony of the march was occasionally relieved by a tune on the drums or fifes, or, oftener, by someone singing a song with a good chorus, in which all joined, doubtlessly scaring many a wild denizen of the jungle, who probably wondered—if they could wonder—the cause of such, to them,, unearthly yelling. When about half way on a day's march, we found coffee and biscuits waiting for us by the roadside. A cup of coffee and a biscuit, and off we trudged again till we came to the camp, pitched the tents,, and afterwards rambled about the country, or slept, as we felt disposed.

The chief pleasure in marching, to me, consisted in the perpetual change of scenery, the whole line of march forming, as it were, a vast panoramic view, of which each day developed some new phase or beauty, and the details of which I traced out, as well as I could, in my own private rambles. At one time in the heart of a vast jungle, at another amid cornfields, now under a beautiful *tope* of mango-trees, on the banks of a broad river, by the side of some mountain, on the open plain; changes every day; towns, villages, mosques, temples, and bridges in endless variety, to say nothing of the meeting with all sorts of strange faces and stranger costumes, queer-equipages with queerer occupants. Here I must record the truthfulness and fidelity of description of a favourite boot. I recognised and could point out every one of the characters in the *Arabian Nights' Entertainments, dervishes, calenders,* everyone, from the Caliph Haroun Al Raschid down to the barber; and I could take my solemn oath I have met the old *dervish* leading off the string of camels loaded with treasure after the covetous man had blinded himself by applying the ointment to both his eyes. I have felt positive in my own mind, too, that I have passed the very ravine leading to the Peri Banao's palace.

On one occasion an attack was made by a party of us on a native village, the inhabitants of which having beaten one of the men, a number of us sallied out with tent-pegs, mallet-handles, &c., and gallantly stormed the mud walls, utterly routing the natives. but almost immediately after, ignominiously retreating ourselves at the approach of the guard who had turned out in force to stay hostilities if possible, or seize delinquents. Some few stragglers were taken, and eventually got punished for the whole.

On another occasion the column, while on the march one morning before daylight, was suddenly startled by the cry "A tiger! a tiger!" There was instantly a commotion in the ranks, and through the darkness the creature came bounding along, scattering everyone right and left, into the jungle, some even climbing trees in their desire to escape the fangs and claws of the much-dreaded monster. This tiger turned out, after all, to be a young bullock, which had been tied behind one of the *hackeries*, but evincing a misanthropical disposition, and displaying a tendency to use both hoof and horn on the passer-by, he had been goaded with the stick of each man who passed, till, almost maddened, it finally broke loose, plunged through the column, getting the credit of being a tiger, and had it all his own way till recaptured.

Tigers at some places on the road, however, were pretty plentiful; at one halting-ground a *bheestie* was carried off bodily by one of them in broad daylight, and within a few hundred yards of the camp. At places, too, in the jungle the men on guard were supplied with firewood, and their principal duty consisted in keeping up large fires all round the camp to prevent tigers or other wild animals from entering. I remember on one occasion being on night-duty, and I must confess to a feeling of nervousness when left alone at my post about midnight. Total silence in camp, everyone buried in profound sleep, sentries, in the strong glare of the watch-fires, flitting backwards and forwards, or tending the fires like fire-fiends; beyond, out in the jungle, intensely black, and rendered, if possible, still more so by the near light of the fires.

I took good care to keep a good blazing fire, also to remain on the side nearest the tents, with my ear stretched to catch the faintest sound from without. The crackling of a twig, a falling leaf, would make me start and hold my breath, fancying swarms of tigers were about, awaiting only an opportunity when the fire should get lower to pounce on me and carry me off. This sort of thing was occasionally varied by a distant roar or a growl, seemingly so near that the very blood curdled in my veins; but the most abominable sound of all was the laugh of the hyena. This I heard several times, and I don't feel the slightest inclination to hear it again; for anything more diabolical, Satanic, sardonic—I am at a loss for expletives—it would be impossible to imagine. It appears as if a fiend were busily engaged torturing some unfortunate victim, and now and then leaving off to indulge in a mocking laugh at his sufferings, the laugh terminating in a sort of ironical snigger. It is beyond the power of my pen to convey anything but the faintest idea of that unearthly laugh. I was very glad when the time came to be relieved and I could curl myself up on the ground in the guard-tent and dream of Mem instead.

Some of our *mahouts*, while going through the jungle, managed to catch a she-elephant and her young one. The young one, about three feet in height, naturally followed its dam, and was the source of much amusement. I saw it one morning as we were sitting down to breakfast on the ground in the open air—our tents not yet having come up—slowly steal up behind the brief-speaking old soldier, deliberately butt him over, snatch up his loaf, and, with trunk erect, trot off with it, actually roaring with laughter—if an elephant can laugh—at the feat, eliciting from the surprised veteran the unusually long sentence, "Well, I'm blarmed! that young swine has bolted off with my *roti*."

I had often heard and read of the intelligence of the elephant, but I had not the remotest idea of the estimation in which they are held in India, or the amount of intelligence they display, and was not at all prepared for what I now heard and saw. On one occasion I saw an elephant tried by a court-martial for killing his keeper. The whole of the keepers and elephants were assembled beneath a large tree, the prisoner, with his fore legs chained, was placed in the midst. The keepers, after discussing the particulars of the case, and unanimously agreeing in the verdict, uttered his sentence aloud to the surrounding elephants, who seemed to acquiesce in its justice.

The sentence was: "That he should receive fifty lashes, have his grog stopped for a month, and wear a distinguishing badge, in the shape of a chain, for the like period." He was at once chained up to the tree, and a veteran elephant advanced to the front and administered the fifty lashes with a chain, to the evident disgust of the culprit and the edification of the surrounding elephants, who were solemnly looking on. The old fellow whirled both chain and trunk round in a manner that showed he was an adept in the science of flogging, and the victim, beyond wincing and grunting, bearing the punishment like a—a—an elephant. The worst part of it, however, was yet to come—the stoppage of his grog—for, strange as it may seem, I learnt that at that time each elephant had his daily allowance of grog, much in the same manner as the men, but with the quantity in proportion to their size. He would consequently daily feel the deprivation of his favourite beverage for a month. I often saw him during the period swinging gracefully along, trailing a stout chain to his forelegs.

Elephants have a keen sense of the ridiculous; they do not like to be made the subject of a joke themselves, but they enjoy one at another's expense immensely. I afterwards had daily opportunities of observing this, as an elephant belonged to my tent. Each elephant, in addition to other forage, has a daily allowance of meat, which is manufactured into cakes for him by the keeper under his own immediate superintendence, and he will take care that he is not mulcted of any of his allowance, weighing every cake that is made in his trunk.

I have seen my particular elephant watch his opportunity, and when the keeper has been looking in another direction, stealthily abstract a cake and place it with his trunk on the top of his head, where, of course, it would be out of sight; and it was really a treat to watch the air of gravity he assumed, and the merry twinkle of his comical little eyes when he saw the consternation of the keeper at missing a cake. This same elephant nursed the keeper's child while the mother was occupied cooking, &c., and no nurse in the world could display more solicitude, or nurse a babe more tenderly than he used to, rocking it to sleep as gently and securely in his trunk as if it were in a cradle.

At length we arrived in Meerut—which the milestone told us was 999 miles from Calcutta—a place so often described in the various accounts of the Mutiny that a description from my pen would be superfluous. Here the depôt of the 14th Dragoons was ordered to remain, and the remainder of the depôts started off again the next morning for stations further up the country. In a few days we were gratified by seeing the regiment march in, embrowned by exposure and hard service in the field, having just come from the Sikh War; and proud we were of belonging to such a fine body of men, and anxious for the time when we could turn out in all the panoply of war like them. We were at once marched out on the parade-ground, inspected by the colonel, lots were drawn for us by the captains of troops, and our depôt, as a depôt, was no more; we were distributed to the different troops, my destination being the H Troop of H.M.'s. 14th Light Dragoons.

CHAPTER 5

Meerut

"Now, then, which are you going to keep?" The taciturn old soldier had just returned from a sharp field day, hungry as a hunter after his morning's ride, when on entering his quarters and expecting to find a breakfast already laid for his particular behoof, he found his wife be-nightcapped and snugly ensconced on the bed with two little mites of babies as snugly nestling in her bosom. He was certainly more surprised than delighted when he was congratulated by the matrons present as the happy father of these two precious darlings. "Such ducks too!" ejaculated one of them—"the innercent little lambs, quite a pidging pair, ain't they?" triumphantly turning down a bit of the counterpane to exhibit them.

The father, perhaps, could not perceive the beauty either of the metaphor or of "the innercent little lambs," but thought they looked remarkably red. Nor could he see the affinity between a pair of squalling bantlings and such tender comestibles as ducks, lambs, or "pidgings," beyond the tenderness part. Worlds would not have induced him to touch one of them "for fear of breaking 'em," as he afterwards remarked. Looking at the officious but kind- hearted women more in sorrow than in anger—without a word—but with sadness depicted on his manly brow, he strode forth.

Five—nay, two minutes had hardly elapsed when he returned bending beneath the weight of a heavy burden, and gave vent to the expression that ornaments the head of this chapter. "Now, then, which are you going to keep?" repeated he, placing his burden on the ground, and looking round complacently on the assembled company, as if conscious that he was making so liberal an offer that it could not fail to be appreciated.

"Why, good gracious!" exclaimed one of the women, "what has he

29

brought that here for?" That alluded to by the woman was the burden he had just deposited on the ground, *a bucket of cold water*. "What does the man mean? Does he think he's a going to drownd these 'ere precious babes as if they wos puppy-dogs, or wot?"

"Look'ee here," exclaimed the taciturn old soldier, and, meeting the exigencies of the case, he for once threw off his taciturnity and became quite eloquent and grand in his eloquence, "Look'ee here, I aint't a going, you know, to have *two* babbies a-knocking about the place. I never bargained for two, and I'm damned if I'm a-going to have two, I don't mind breedin' one on 'em, but when it comes to two—why—I—I ain't agreeable, so that's all about it. However, you shan't say I'm acting shabby, for you shall have your pick—whichever one you like. Now, then, make your choice, cos the other" A significant glance at the bucket was more expressive than mere words, and rounded the sentence off admirably. "As I said afore, which are you a-going to keep?" He was interrupted in a fresh burst of eloquence by a regular *feu-de-joie* of abuse from the assembled matrons. We often hear of a volley of abuse, but a *feu-de-joie* is infinitely more effective; a volley is over, or supposed to be over, at one grand discharge, but a *feu-de-joie* is a running fire—if one shot misses, another is sure to tell.

"You unnateral monster! do you think your own flesh and blood is pups, or wot?" said one.

"If I had my will," said another, "it's *you* that should be drownded in that there bucket instead of them blessed babes"—which, considering his size, would have been rather a difficult undertaking.

In the midst of this desultory fire, the old soldier was glad to beat a hasty retreat; while the mother, who knew him better than any of them, exclaimed:

"Lor' bless you, you mustn't mind *him*—that's onny his way, he *will* have his joke. He *drownd* either of these little darlings! Not much! I'll bet anything now, if you could onny see him, that he's laffing fit to crack his sides—onny he don't show it—he keeps his laffs inside on him; but for all his looking so serous—if you knowed him as well as I do, you would say he's the funniest man you ever met, and the kindest too—why he wouldn't hurt a worm, would he, my precious ones?" Here she addressed her conversation particularly to the new comers,—much to their edification—in the way that mothers do talk to their babies.

These few remarks, however, somewhat mollified the matrons, and they began to entertain different views as to his intentions towards the children; but they did not fail to mention the incident to their various friends, and the old soldier was often greeted in a jocular way by his comrades, with the now standard joker popular inquiry, "Well, which are you going to keep?"

In the meantime I was progressing very rapidly with my drills, both foot and mounted, and in due time I was dismissed recruit drill, and, being considered a smart soldier, was at once put into the first class and "told off" as a regular skirmisher, which, unless a man has a first-rate horse, steady under fire, and that will obey the slightest move of hand or leg, is not by any means an enviable position, a spirited or vicious horse often getting his rider extra drill. However, I can boast that in a period of twelve years I never did one days' extra drill, either for my horse or myself, which is saying a great deal for both parties.

I was at that time very fond of dancing, so I at once became a member of several of the dances held in the regiment, and, being an adept in "the poetry of motion," was shortly after elected to the responsible office of M.C. of the weekly dance held in my own troop. These dances were comparatively costless, there being nothing but tea, coffee, or lemonade allowed. Being almost the only amusement the women of the regiment could indulge in, they were looked forward to as a positive treat. These dances, too, had a sort of civilising influence on the men, occasional contact with the softer sex at these social gatherings having a softening effect on their rougher natures, and reminding them that, though far from home, they were not altogether without the pale of civilisation. They were, besides, conducted as respectably as the most fashionable balls at home could be, and were, no doubt, quite as much enjoyed. I look back to them with pleasure.

Sometimes, too, they had their absurd side; for instance, one evening an old woman belonging to the regiment, who had probably never before danced in her life, was persuaded by a mischievous fellow to stand up with him in the "Lancers," the individual in question assuring her it was the simplest thing in the world, and that she had only to watch his movements and imitate them.

Thus assured, the old lady confidently stood up with him, they taking one of the sides. The music struck up, and, instructed by her partner, she went through the initiatory bowing to perfection; immediately the gentleman, with a face as grave as a judge, commenced a "cellar-flap," working both arms and legs in the most approved fashion, occasionally smiling benignantly on those opposite, whom politeness only kept from roaring with laughter; the old lady, with an agility worthy of a better cause, did the same, making frantic attempts at a "double-shuffle" to bear him company, also smiling complacently as she saw him do. Fortunately it came to their turn in reality to dance, and the old lady was led triumphantly through the figure; she had previously been hoaxed, utterly unconscious of the hoax that had been practised on her, and imagining she had made her *debût* in dancing with great *éclat*.

Chapter 6

"Now say that"

"Now say that."

The person appealed to *did* say that, whatever it was, and instantly a simultaneous roar of laughter burst from, seven hundred throats.

"Ho! ho! ho! ha! ha! ha! hi! hi! hi!"

The parties alluded to in the foregoing were—a corporal of the 1st Fusiliers; Corporal O'Niel of the 14th Dragoons, commonly called Pat O'Niel, unless on duty, when he exacted the title due to his rank; and the laughers.

The laughers were *horses*.

The laughter was continued in every tone of voice, from the deep bass guffawy horse-laugh to the treble whinnying giggle. The owners of the seven hundred throats, independent of their derisive laughter, exhibited their merriment in a variety of fantastic ways, such as snorting, pawing, biting, kicking, bucking, jumping, plunging, rearing, &c, and were only restrained in their merriment by the strong head and heel ropes that kept them within due bounds.

"Ha! ha! ha! ho! ho! ho! hi! hi! hi!"

"Glory be to God, but *that* bangs Banaghar!" ejaculated the speaker of *that*.

"Well, do you give in that you've lost?" inquired the other.

"Is it lost ye mane? Throth, thin, it's meself that's lost intirely!" They returned to the barrack room.

What was the cause of this uproarious merriment amongst the horses, and what was the *that* that caused it? I will tell you.

Corporal Mynn had that morning strolled down to our lines on a friendly visit to Pat O'Niel, and even at that early hour they had imbibed a few "drops of the cratur." Now Pat was a harem-scarem devil-may-care sort of a fellow, a perfect gentleman in manner when

33

he chose to be so, when he could spit out the brogue with the wildest Irishman breathing; he was withal brimful of wit and humour, and was perpetually up to some "devilment" or other. During the visit, the pair of them had been busily engaged discussing the various merits of infantry and cavalry—the one stoutly maintaining the infantry was the best service, the other as enthusiastically upholding the cavalry. After a long argument on the subject Corporal Flynn exclaimed:

"Throth, thin, ye may prate about yer horse, an yer sword, an yer spikes, but I'll stick to Brown Bess; an' I say that the infantry is better than the cavalry."

"Hould yer whist!" exclaimed Pat, "don't be blathering that way! Why, man, if you was to repate thim words out in the lines, every mother's son of the horses would laugh at yer; an' I'm game to bet ye a bottle on the strength of it."

The bet was arranged, and the two proceeded to the horse-lines accompanied by others to witness the ceremony. Pat had artfully managed it so that they left the room just as the clock was on the point of twelve, knowing the horses were fed at that time, and at the first blast of the trumpet for "feed" would neigh and fret with impatience till they got their corn. He saw the trumpeter in the distance raise the trumpet to his mouth to sound, he confidently invited the corporal to say *that*, and the latter at once repeated the asseveration "I say that the infantry is better than the cavalry," with the result as described above.

I cannot resist here giving another specimen of Pat's wit and his pardonable vanity, or rather the *esprit du corps* displayed by him. One day some athletic sports were going on at the back of the lines, and Pat, who was an athlete, had managed to carry off two or three prizes, and was consequently elated at his success. His part in the programme being over, he had donned his uniform, and was sauntering homeward, when he encountered an infantry officer in mufti, whom, of course, he passed without saluting. The officer, piqued at this, called him back, and asked why he did not salute him. Pat replied by his not being in uniform he thought he was not an officer, and politely inquired his name and rank that he might know him in future. The officer innocently gave both, he turning out to be a lieutenant. Pat immediately exclaimed, "It appears, then, that you ought to have saluted me instead of my saluting you. Do you know that I'm your superior officer? especially as I am in regimentals, which makes it all the more inexcusable in you." The officer began to fancy he had rather a strange character to deal with; but wishing to know a little more about Pat, and being himself a bit of a wag, he said he should like to be enlightened as to how a corporal could be superior in rank to a lieutenant.

"Well, then, I'll tell you," said Pat. "A private dragoon ranks with a field officer in the infantry, because none under that rank are allowed to wear spurs or ride a horse on parade, and a private dragoon does both. Now I'm a corporal of dragoons, consequently your superior officer." The officer instead of being foolishly angry, was extremely amused at Pat's ingenious reasoning, and showed it by sending him a case of brandy that evening, which Pat duly shared among his admiring comrades, at the same time gleefully recounting the adventure which led to such a liberal gift.

CHAPTER 7

Theatrical Reminiscences

Having always had a taste for theatricals, I made application to become a member of the "Dramatic Corps" belonging to the regiment, and was placed at once on the probationary list till the body of amateurs could decide on my capabilities. I made my debût—a double-breasted one, as a friend facetiously observed—shortly afterwards on the stage of the Station Theatre, playing the character of Seaweed in *Black-eyed Susan*, and singing a comic nigger melody between the pieces, accompanying myself on the bones. I think I may venture to say I was the first European that introduced that delectable style of singing and music on the boards in India. I repeat it emphatically—music. For that there is music in the bones I had ample proof; that is, if there is any truth in the well-known lines—

Music hath charms to soothe the savage breast, &c.

for I nightly soothed the savage breast of a *cobra-di-capello*, and it isn't often a singer has a *cobra-di-capello* for an audience. It occurred in this wise. Being engaged to sing the above-mentioned nigger melody, with bone accompaniment, a certain amount of practice was required, and I am free to admit that however melodious that sort of music might be at times, one does not care to have it constantly ringing in his ears; so to avoid annoying anyone, I used to walk out of an evening on the plain, about a mile away from the lines, sit down on the brink of a ruined well, and rattle away to my heart's content, grimacing meanwhile like a maniac. It was a bright moonlight night the first time I went, and I was sitting on the edge of the well, bringing out a particular roll I required, when I saw a few yards in front of me what I took to be a long pole. I paid no attention to this, but continued my practice.

Shortly after, happening to look in that direction again, I fancied it appeared a good deal nearer. "Devilish strange," thought I. While staring intently at this phenomenon—still going on with the bones—I became conscious of an almost imperceptible movement on the part of the pole towards me, but so slowly as scarcely to be observed. However, I still continued playing—at the same time watching carefully this object, when I felt convinced it was a snake—and by this time I had been long enough in the country to know how to distinguish a common "carpet-snake," which is harmless, from a "cobra," whose bite is fatal. I, therefore, detached a piece of brick from the edge of the well, and tossed it towards the pole, when, with a succession of hisses, it raised itself erect in a moment, and darted at me, thus proving it to be a "cobra," for a "carpet-snake" on being thrown at would have been as ready to retire as the cobra was to attack.

I need not say that I practised no more that night; but the next night, after carefully looking round to see that he was not near the edge of the well, I took up the same position as I had the previous night, and commenced practice, with precisely the same result—the snake appearing as before, and gradually drawing nearer till within about four yards distance, when he remained stationary and apparently highly delighted with my performance, as he never made any attempt to meddle with me, nor I with him; and for nearly a fortnight I had him nightly for my audience, and although I must admit he never enthusiastically encored or applauded me, yet after the first night he as invariably refrained from hissing me.

Snake-charming has been so often written about, that I can scarcely relate anything concerning it that is new to the reader. Of course, like all Europeans in India, I have seen them dance to the music of the snake-charmer's peculiar pipe, and have also seen the keeper of them allow himself to be bitten by the poisonous reptiles without apparent injury. We, however, had such a hatred of them that we used often to buy one for the express purpose of "hunting it," or rather worrying it, till it became maddened with rage, and, when tired of this strange pastime, killing it.

On one of these occasions a man of my troop had like to have lost his life. We had procured an immense "cobra," and turned him loose on the plain; the reptile on finding himself free began quietly to glide off, but in whatever direction he went he found himself obstructed, each of us being armed with a long stick for that purpose, a thrust of which would excite him, and cause him to make a dart at the offender, which, had he succeeded, would have cost the man his life. Sometimes he would single out one individual, and madly chase him, regardless of the thwacks from the sticks of his tormentors. This snake at length shared the fate of its predecessors by being beaten to death. One of the men took it up by the tail and swung it round his head in triumph; by some means a drop of foam from the mouth of the reptile fell upon the man's hand, in a short time it swelled up to an enormous size. He was immediately taken to hospital, and for a long time his life was despaired of; in fact, he was ill for six months through the effect of that one drop of foam. I mention this incident as showing how deadly their bite must be, if a drop of the poison on the outside of one's skin produces such an effect.

Every animal seems to have an instinctive horror of this much-dreaded reptile, except the mungoose. This daring little animal is the only living thing that will venture to face it. He seems to delight in nothing better than a set-to with this formidable antagonist, in which he invariably comes off victorious. I have seen several fights between the mungoose and the cobra, and although the cobra is perhaps ten times the size of the little fellow, and could swallow him whole, yet such is his agility that he always manages to elude his adversary. The bite of the cobra does not appear to affect him either—or rather there is always an antidote at hand—for when bitten by the cobra the mungoose will run away for a few yards, busily scratch up the ground as if in search of something, and having apparently found what he required, will return again to the conflict, nor desist till he has rendered his foe *hors-de-combat*. What the antidote is—if antidote it be—and there seems no reason to doubt that it is a most potent one, I believe no one has ever been able to discover.

I remember, when I first came into the country, being somewhat scared at the reply of the taciturn old soldier to some question as to what was most necessary for the road. His answer to my inquiry was, "A hammer." By dint of questioning I managed to elicit from him that a "hammer was required the first thing every morning on the road to tap any snakes on the head that might be found under one, and that every recruit ought to have one." I did not fail, after that, to closely scrutinise the ground in and about the tent to look out for snake-holes.

Once, while on sentry in the verandah of the main-guard, a small green snake—well known as being the most deadly kind—either dropped accidentally or jumped purposely from the thatched roof on to my shoulder, startling me considerably. Luckily he fell from thence to the ground, with no other damage to me than the fright. Once on the ground the butt of my carbine became intimately acquainted with his head, effectually putting a stop to any design he might have entertained towards me.

The most curious kind of snake I ever saw is the "double-headed" snake. This is from two to three feet long, nearly the thickness of one's wrist, and not much unlike a bludgeon. On closely inspecting it, it will be found to have one end acting for the time being as head, "properly fitted up" with all the requirements for eating, &c.; but the other end, acting as tail, and a facsimile of the head, appears to be hermetically sealed. The natives say it uses either end as head and tail alternately, changing every six months. Thus, at the end of six months the closed-up end, that has answered the purpose of tail for that period, opens and becomes the head, while the head in turn closes up and becomes the tail, and so on. I confess this is a subject rather beyond my comprehension, and I cannot call to mind ever reading any scientific explanation of this singular phenomenon. The snake, however, is very common and easily procurable. I feel sure any naturalist would merit the thanks, of the scientific world at least, if he could, either by keeping one and daily watching it, or by some other process, arrive at some satisfactory reason for this curious freak of nature. Perhaps—nay, let me trust that my few remarks on the subject may induce someone to endeavour to elucidate the mystery connected with the "double-headed snake."

Well, I declare! if I have not imperceptibly glided, like my quondam friend the cobra, from theatricals into the history of snakes, or something very closely approaching it. Yet there may be some slight affinity between the two, for I *have* seen one or two of our best players who have died "seeing snakes," and brought to it by drink.—a slower poison sometimes, but in India often as rapid as the bite of the deadly cobra.

To return to my original subject: I gave such satisfaction at my *debût* in theatricals, that I was promoted to the third class at the next meeting of amateurs, and the conclusion of two more plays saw me ranked as a first-class player, and I ultimately became stage-manager, which position I filled till I left the regiment; but of this more hereafter.

CHAPTER 8

Theatricals in Earnest

I was soon discovered to be so versatile in my proclivities that I was cast for any important character—man, woman, old, young, dramatic or comic, were given to me indiscriminately. The reader may form some idea of the variety when I state that in *Green Bushes* I have personated the character of Old Meg the blacksmith's wife and Master Grinnidge in one night, and at another time "Nelly O'Neill" in the same piece. Those familiar with theatricals will readily perceive the marked contrast between those three characters.

Sometimes during a performance many of the officers came behind the scenes, when they were, if not regular visitors, "chalked," which meant a case of brandy or beer. I have even seen a "chit" given for six dozen of brandy, which is paying rather dear for the privilege of going behind the scenes. The "chits" were kept till the day after the performance, when the whole of the amateurs and the theatrical *employés* would adjourn to the riding-school and discuss the produce of these chits, much to their satisfaction, the meeting often proving a regular orgie—the "speechless ones," as they dropped off, being carefully laid in a row in one corner by their more sober comrades.

One day we had so much drink on hand that, wishing to get rid of some of it, I, unknown to the remainder, got two dozen bottles, opened them, and emptied them into the "water *chattie*" kept for the use of those attending riding-school when they were thirsty. The next morning there was a squad at riding-drill, and one of them asked permission to fall out for a drink of water: to his intense surprise and gratification he found, instead of the pure beverage as he anticipated, good strong brandy-and-water in the "*chattie*." Taking a hearty swig or two he returned to his place, communicating the important fact to the men on either side of him, who also asked leave to "fall out," and, after paying their respects to the *chattie*, returning and telling others in like manner. This sort of thing continued till the whole ride knew of it, and were constantly asking to fall out, and as constantly returning smacking their lips and looking redder in the face after each visit.

The sergeant noticing these symptoms, and thinking it very strange there should be such an unusual demand for water, determined to go himself and ascertain its cause if possible. He soon discovered what attracted them, and he and his ride plied the *chattie* so well that they got chatty themselves; and one or two, not content with "falling out," must needs "fall off"; and the end of it was several found themselves, on waking up from a drunken sleep, incarcerated in durance vile.

About this time, if I remember rightly, the station was visited by the King of Gwalior—then quite a lad—the governor-general, the commander-in-chief, and goodness knows how many other dignitaries; for, as I was not on visiting terms with any of them, I cannot be expected to bear the whole of their names and ranks in my mind. However, the gentlemen amateurs—and the station possessed at the same time two regimental companies—determined to give a grand theatrical entertainment in their honour, none but the *élite* of the station to be admitted, the programmes printed on white satin, and everything done on a scale *magnifique*.

Two days before the performance was to take place, the leading player. Major Geneste, was taken seriously ill, and in this dilemma the stage-manager, the Hon. P. Thesiger, sent for me, requesting me to play Major Geneste's character, Tom Noddy, in *Tom Noddy's Secret*. I undertook to play the part by the time appointed; and before I slept that night I had learnt the whole of the character, and could repeat it without my part.

Now, if I was tender upon any subject in the world, it was theatricals. I may have been conceited—indeed, I know I was—whether or not, I knew that few could surpass me in the personation and playing in any line of character; and, of course, I knew, excepting the original cast, there was no one else who could personate this particular character like me, especially on so short a notice. And, private soldier as I was, I expected some little courtesy to be shown, me, considering I was obliging them. However, at the first rehearsal, which was at night, also a dress one into the bargain, I was treated as if I were a *coolie*, rather, than one supplying the place of their leading player. My costume was thrown to me, and I was directed to dress behind the scenes instead of in the green-room. During that long night not one individual spoke

41

to me except when compelled to address me in the piece; and, although there was a supper laid, not a soul asked me whether I wanted refreshments or not. I did not care for drink, and never drank on the nights of play, so I was careless as far as that went, but I certainly liked to be asked.

To mend the matter, I was for duty the next morning, and the manager had undertaken to get me relieved from this; but I found in the morning nothing of the sort had been done. I was so utterly disgusted at perceiving I was simply being made a tool of, that I wrote at once to the manager requesting him to get another Tom Noddy, as I would not be one any longer. This quickly brought a visit, and I then told the manager my ideas on the subject:— that though but a private soldier, during the time I was at the theatre playing a leading character I considered myself on the same footing as any member of the corps, no matter what his rank might be; the performance over, or out of the theatre, I was simply a private, and they were officers.

I remained obdurate in spite of the probable disappointment of so fashionable an audience, and at this late period I am afraid I showed some little malice in my refusal to play. The colonel of my regiment, Colonel Doherty, was applied to to coerce me to play; but on hearing my tale, he took my view of the case, and said he would have served them the same for a shabby lot of fellows. I told him, however, if he wished it, or ordered me to play, I would do it at either his wish or order.

"No," said he, "I will not influence you in any way. I should have done the same myself had I been in your place."

"Then, sir," I replied, "if you don't order me, I won't play"; and, careless whoever might have composed the audience, I did not, and the performance could not come off at the time appointed.

About a month after this a very similar case occurred. Curiously enough, another leading player was taken sick a day or two before the play. Recourse was had to me again, I being requested to take his character—that of "Appleface" in the *Catspaw*—and it was something amusing to see the marked difference in their behaviour to me. Everyone was polite, and I was constantly invited to imbibe. I had a proper place to dress in—in fact, nothing was too good for me. Knowing this was but the effect of my former withdrawal at a critical moment, I appreciated it for what it was worth. I could not resist, however, occasionally displaying some of my satirical wit at the expense of a little officer in the native infantry who would make himself officious about me,. and who, having about five words to say, assumed all the airs of a "star."

"But," said he, on one occasion, "you are playing the character of an infantry drummer, and you wear an imperial. I thought the cavalry were not allowed to wear one?"

This was touching me in a tender place, for I had surreptitiously nurtured the incipient budding of an imperial, which under my careful management and tender treatment had gradually developed.

"No," I replied, "we are not supposed to wear them, but I like to be a little different from the infantry; and since they have taken to wearing the moustache, I indulge in an imperial."

Another time, at a dress rehearsal, he came up to me and said:

"Why, your drummer's chevrons are bottom upwards!"

"Are they?" I remarked. "Well, *you* may understand that sort of thing, but as I don't associate much with foot-soldiers, I haven't the remotest idea which way they ought to be."

These sallies would elicit roars of laughter from the bystanders, and for a short time rather embarrass the little officer, who would, however, shortly after make another attack, only to sustain another repulse. I must say, though, that, deducting his consequential ways, he was not a bad little fellow at bottom. To cut the matter short, the play was a success, and I never after had occasion to complain of want of politeness on the part of the "gentlemen amateurs."

Chapter 9

"I Love You"

"I love you!"

Somehow or other, I could not resist the impulse to utter the above impassioned exclamation.

I had waylaid the fairy-like little being to whom I addressed it on her road back from the Catholic Chapel, and was escorting her part of the way home, as I often used to do, meeting her always, of course, accidentally.

On this particular morning the sun shone so pleasantly, the trees and flowers seemed to possess an additional beauty, the air was redolent with fragrance, the very birds seemed to be twittering "I love you" to each other, and she looked so bewitching as she walked by my side, that, for the life of me, I felt I had no alternative but saying so too.

"I love you," I repeated; for at first she seemed as much "taken aback" at hearing such an expression as I was surprised at myself for giving utterance to it. However, having broken the ice, I followed up the attack by blurting out an incoherent string of nonsense all tending the same way, when I was brought to a full stop by the simple words "Mr. ——!"

The mere utterance of those two words, or, rather, their peculiar intonation, conveyed volumes of reproach. "Is this your return for our kindness?" continued she, drawing her little form up as majestically as a queen. "Do you think my mother would have allowed you to visit us if she thought you would have repaid her by insulting her daughter? Go!" cried she, stamping her little foot on the road. "Go! and never come to our place again!"

Here was a pretty kettle of fish! Entreaties for forgiveness, and promises never to commit myself again, were of no avail; she was inexorable, and pursued her way without condescending to notice a word that I said.

At last, in despair at moving her, I abruptly turned away and strode off in the direction of my lines with what feelings I will leave my readers to imagine, my own impression being that I felt decidedly foolish and crestfallen—for that I *did* love her there was not the slightest doubt, and that I *had* loved her for a long time was equally true; but to give the reader a better idea of the circumstances which led to my avowal of love, and its consequences, I must retrace my steps backwards for a few months.

Mrs. Curran was a widow belonging to the 1st Europeans, her husband having been a sergeant in that corps, but having died, she became a sort of appendage to the regiment till such time as she could either marry again or get her daughter married, and establish herself in her son-in-law's domicile.

As to the former, it was not a very probable contingency, for few would like to be mated with such an old harridan; for, although not yet forty years of age, she looked at least seventy. She was styled, by courtesy, a half-caste, but the black half predominated to a fearful extent, and she might safely have claimed affinity with "the ace of spades," for she was as black as one, and as withered and wrinkled as a mummy.

Black, ugly, and wrinkled as the mother was, many a young fellow tried to get into her good graces for the sake of her daughter, who was just as plump and fair as her mother was the reverse. To see them together no one would for a moment imagine that they were mother and daughter, so utterly different were they in every way.

Rose—that was her name—was such a wilful, wicked, conceited, pouting, laughing, bright-eyed little pet, that one could not avoid falling in love with her; for if she annoyed you mischievously one moment, the next she would "walk round you" with her winning ways, that there was no resisting her, you felt strongly tempted to seize hold of her and kiss her to death or run away with her as a punishment—at least, I did.

Rose was betrothed to a sergeant of the regiment, who was with it in Burmah on service. It was an understood thing that she was to be married to him the moment the regiment came off the campaign. Knowing this, I was very guarded in my behaviour to her.

I had been for some months past in the habit of visiting at her mother's house, and had been on very friendly terms with Rose; we had even written short notes to each other on occasion of lending books, &c., but not a word of love had ever passed my lips till this unfortunate morning.

Now, however, right or wrong, the ice was broken; I had told her I loved her, with what result the reader has seen.

I reached my quarters and threw myself on my cot, a prey to all sorts of conflicting feelings, cursing my stupidity for being too precipitate, and thereby depriving myself of her society altogether.

It must not be imagined that I had entered on such a proceeding as the above without having had, in my own mind, at least, some little encouragement from the girl herself to almost warrant my making a declaration of love to her with some prospect of success. I could recall many actions on her part which convinced me that I was not altogether distasteful to her; that she even liked—I will not say loved—me. The smile with which my arrival was ever welcomed, the dropping of her eyes when, they encountered mine, and the gentle blush which suffused her face at such times; the pleasure she displayed at everything I said or did, the enjoyment she seemed to experience in my society; the lingering of her hand in mine at parting, accompanied, I could almost swear, sometimes by a gentle pressure; a thousand little nothings in themselves, imperceptible to others, to me were evidences that I had but to tell her I loved her to be at once assured by her own lips that I was, in spite of betrothal to another, not indifferent to her. All these pleasant dreams were now knocked on the head in a moment, owing to my infernal stupidity in not waiting for a proper time and place to tell her I loved her.

I would have given the world to have been able to recall the events of the morning, and continue my visits to her quarters simply as a friend, enjoying the pleasure of her company daily, and keeping my love for her confined to my own breast; but this was all at an end for ever through my blank stupidity.

During the course of the day, while thus brooding over my sorrows, her *ayah* arrived bringing a note and a small parcel of books I had lent her. Even she seemed to sympathise with me, for the expression of her features evidently betrayed that she thought there was something wrong between her mistress and myself; indeed, she hinted as much by a few soothing words, such as "Missee littee cross now, bime-by all brober, *sahib*. No makee too much sorry." I took the letter without saying a word, tore it open, and hastily read the contents, which ran something like this:—

46

Sir,—After what passed between us this morning, I beg you will discontinue your visits to my place, as they must be painful to both of us.

I send you back the presents you have at various times given me, also the books you lent me; and if you have anything of mine, please return it.

I shall account to my mother in the best manner I can for your absence, without mentioning anything of what has occurred.

I *did* have a better opinion of you than to think you would have behaved as you did, knowing how I am situated; but I was mistaken. I can hold out no longer. I do love you, dearly, and I always have, from the first moment I saw you. I ought to have avoided you, I know, when I discovered that I did so, but I foolishly imagined I could be constantly near you, and keep the knowledge of my love to *myself*; or, if we were separated at any time, that neither you nor anyone else would ever know of it. *Now* I know I could not, and I *must* tell you I love you. I could have told you so a thousand times before. Many times, when you, perhaps, have thought I was careless and indifferent, I could have flung my arms round your neck and told you how dearly I loved you. Come again this evening as usual, as if those cruel words of mine had never been uttered, as if you had just said 'I love you' and were waiting for a reply; and be assured, reckless of betrothal, of all, my answer shall be, both by my lips and every action of my life, the echo of those dear words of yours,—'I love you.'

CHAPTER 10

Dummy

Hoo-hoo-hoo-oo-oo-o-o!

Startled by such a diabolical yell, or rather series of yells, Rose and I hastily looked up from our employment to ascertain the cause of it, and beheld a fat old woman frantically gesticulating at us; beating her breast, kissing her fingers, and going through a variety of pantomime with her fingers and hands. The old woman was deaf and dumb.

Rose and I had been comfortably seated at table, pleasantly occupied in "making love under difficulties," by writing on slips of paper and passing them to each other, as if they contained extracts from various poets, when in reality we were mating all sorts of vows of love to each other under cover of that process.

The old lady, her mother, was busily plying her needle, and as she was entirely innocent of any knowledge of reading or writing, she would have remained in blissful ignorance of our pleasant mode of passing the time, but for the untimely arrival of the deaf and dumb woman, or, as she was called, "the Dummy," Mrs. Macgaverin.

Knowing her to be deaf and dumb, we naturally thought she must also not be able to understand reading or writing. We, therefore, pursued our interesting occupation utterly indifferent whether "Dummy" was there or not, till, startled by her yelling, and seeing her antics, we began to form some idea that it was just possible for a "dummy" to read and also to *tell*. This we soon found out to our sorrow.

She had been intently watching us for some time, and had seen enough to convince her that we were making violent love to each other, right under the eyes of the unsuspicious mother, without her knowledge or sanction, and at once conceived it her duty to make the mother acquainted with such a breach of confidence.

Mrs. Macgaverin rapidly manipulated her fingers, and gave, no

48

doubt, an eloquent account of our little game at calligraphy, to the horror and anger of the mother of Rose, who, without more ado, ordered me out of the place, with a very pressing desire that I would not fatigue myself by again venturing there. Of course, I had no alternative, and I retired from the scene of my poetical effusions somewhat crest-fallen; as for Rose, finding pleading was of no avail, she had recourse to tears, and in that state I left her undergoing a lecture from her indignant mother.

Being prohibited from seeing each other at the girl's quarters, we naturally (however wrongly) endeavoured to devise some expedient so that we might meet at other places without the knowledge of her mother.

Rose, as I mentioned in the last chapter, had an *ayah*, and, seeing no other help for it, took this girl into her confidence, and she assisted us materially by being the means of communication between us, bringing me two or three *billet-doux* daily, and receiving a similar number in return, which she faithfully conveyed to her young mistress.

In this manner a plan was arranged so that I should at least be able to see her daily. It was this:—the Catholic priest was organising a choir of singers for his chapel, and, being an energetic character, he managed to collect many recruits from the different regiments stationed at Meerut, and among them were upwards of a dozen women and girls. Rose being a Catholic, I easily persuaded her to become one of the singers—fully bent on being one myself eventually. I, therefore, obtained a prayer-book from her, and at once set to work to learn the whole of the Latin for the different services. This task, inspired by love, I accomplished in a very few days.

My next plan was to get *invited* to join the singers; for I, as a Protestant, could not reasonably go and ask to be admitted among them as a singer only. I thought this over for a long time; at length I fancied I could see my way clear how it might be done, and I hastened to put my plan into practice.

One evening I entered the chapel in plain clothes while they were at practice, sat down in a prominent place close by them, directly in front of the priest, and prepared to listen to the singing, having at the same time an eye to the success of my plan. All eyes were naturally turned on me (those of Rose in particular), for they could tell I was not a regular visitant. The singing proceeded; and, of course, having but recently commenced practising, there was occasionally a little discord, which I took care to show I noticed by fidgeting when it occurred. The priest I observed was not slow in perceiving that I did so, which was just the thing I wanted. I repeated this process for several evenings, till the priest got quite into the habit of looking towards me as if watching for my approval or disapproval. In the meanwhile I was not wasting my time, for, having a quick ear for music, I learnt the tunes of the different hymns and chants very rapidly; but apparently taking no notice of Rose, nor speaking to a soul there.

One evening, after they had practised for some time, the priest came up to me and said, "Young man, I have noticed that you have regularly attended our practices for the last seven or eight evenings, and when there has been any little discord, I could see by your manner that you detected it. Perhaps, as you seem to take such an interest in our singing, you might be induced to join us, and give us the advantage of your voice as well as your presence."

I told him that having accidentally passed the chapel while the singing was going on one evening, I had entered out of curiosity, attracted by the music; since then I had attended purely from the pleasure of listening to it. I added, I should be most happy to assist, but I was afraid there was an insuperable objection to it—in fact, that I was a Protestant.

"Don't let that be an obstacle," he replied, "anything in such a cause, no matter whether it comes from a Protestant or Catholic, will be acceptable."

"At that rate," I answered, "I shall be most happy to assist."

He, having first ascertained I could sing a second, but little thinking I knew every note and word of the service, requested me to accompany him in the *Lucis Creator Optime*. First glancing my eye to where Rose sat, to give me confidence, and to let her see that it should not be my fault if my plan did not succeed, I sang my best, and acquitted myself so creditably, that the priest expressed himself highly delighted with my singing, and congratulated himself on the acquisition my voice would be to the choir, having no suspicion what a wolf in sheep's clothing he was turning loose into his fold.

I was henceforth installed as one of the singers, and passed many pleasant hours among them, always managing to be near Rose, and seeing her to the "lines" in which her mother's quarters were, every evening. This agreeable state of things did not last many weeks, for it, unfortunately, came to her mother's ears, and Rose was not allowed to go to the chapel any more unless accompanied by the old lady. I was thus deprived of my pleasant evenings, the choir of a voice, and Rose of my escort back every evening.

Our next plan for meeting was as follows:—Rose, at my instigation, pretended sickness, and was sent to the hospital, and I made the acquaintance of a motherly old lady of the 81st Foot, to whom I related my love for the girl, begging her assistance so far as to allow me to keep a woman's outfit in her quarters so that I might be able to disguise myself there, and from thence sally forth, as a female, and visit Rose in hospital.

The old lady, after hearing my story, hugged me round the neck, and exclaimed, "I wish I was a girl and you were running after me, you shouldn't have to run far, nor disguise yourself neither, for I'd run after you, in spite of all the mothers in the world." Of course, I felt flattered.

She gave the required permission at once, fitted up nails for me to hang my female fixings on, and every evening, with the sanction of her husband, who used to look on admiringly when I was fully equipped as a lady, she assisted me in dressing, gave me a hearty kiss and a blessing, and sent me out on my adventures.

There were several women in the hospital as well as Rose, but confident in my disguise and thorough knowledge of the "business" required of me as a female—for which I must thank my theatrical training—I fearlessly ventured among them, freely gossiping with them, when circumstances compelled me, often sitting with three or four of them on the bed, chatting on various subjects, without so much as their entertaining the slightest suspicion but that I was a *bonâ fide* woman belonging to another regiment.[1] This, however, lasted only for about a fortnight, for the doctor discharged her from the hospital as *recovered*, he, perhaps, by this time finding out there was really nothing the matter with her, or she not being able to "scheme"[2] any longer.

A variety of plans were arranged after this, and I used, to go in all sorts of disguises to snatch a few moments in her company of an

---

1. This was easily managed; the lines occupied by the depôt of the 1st Europeans were also occupied by the depôt of the 18th Royal Irish, the 81st Foot, and some artillery. The women's hospital I allude to was for the women and children of the above corps only. The lines of the 14th were about a mile distant; the women of the 14th had their own hospital. I could, therefore, pass myself off easily as a woman of the latter, and, knowing every woman in the regiment, could readily answer any question that might be put to me on any subject without danger of being discovered. I have mixed with the women under more peculiar circumstances still, and never—fortunately for me—was even suspected.
2. Pretend sickness.

evening.[3] But all our schemes of happiness were abruptly put a stop to by a sudden order for the depôt of the 1st Europeans to proceed at once to Dinapore to join the regiment, which had already left Burmah and was *en route* for that place.

I will not attempt to describe our separation; it was painful on both sides; nor should she have gone, for I would have risked everything, but that my regiment was also under orders to march to Bombay, and from thence proceed to the Crimea, so that there was no help for it.

I never saw her afterwards; but on arriving at Kirkee, I received a letter from her, saying she was now free, her betrothed being dead; giving me some account of his death, which occurred under peculiar circumstances, which

I may as well relate.

It seems the depôt from Meerut, in which Rose was proceeding to Dinapore, and the regiment from Burmah, in which was her betrothed, also proceeding thither, were each one day's distance from Dinapore in opposite directions, and must consequently meet the next day. The young man was somewhat of a sportsman, and seeing an alligator in the river, a short distance from the steamer, he got his gun and fired at it. In doing so, he over-reached himself and tumbled into the water, and the probability is that he became food for the monster he had intended to shoot, for he never rose again, while the alligator was seen to dive under as if in pursuit of a meal. This accident left Rose free, in consequence of which she at once wrote to me, thinking now all obstacles were removed to our union.

Filled with hope at such a bright prospect, I wrote off at once, telling her that our departure for the Crimea was countermanded, the war having come to a close; that I should only be too happy to make

---

3. It may not be amiss here to show what power priests wield over their flocks. I used often to go in disguise to the chapel, among other places, and was undetected invariably; but, for some reason or other Rose went to confession one Saturday afternoon, and, of course, made a clean breast of it. In the evening I met her, and, to my surprise, was received very coolly. I could plainly perceive she had been influenced against me by someone; but all my inquiries failed to elicit satisfactory replies, till, it suddenly striking me it was Saturday—confession day—I taxed her with having been to confession, and that the priest had caused this change in her demeanour. After some few struggles she told me she had been to confession, and that the priest had refused her absolution. She was to have no correspondence with me in any shape or form, and come back at the end of a week and confess again, when the priest would, if he thought her deserving of it, give her absolution. It may easily be conceived by this, how they may influence females for either good or bad purposes. Often the latter, as I have had opportunities of knowing.

her mine now that all obstacles were removed, and would send for her as soon as I received an answer from her, letting me know how I could best manage it, and that, I would apply for permission at once.

I waited anxiously, but no answer came. I wrote again and again till I was nearly distracted, but with the same result. At length, concluding that she had thrown me aside for some more favoured individual, I gave way to despair, and discontinued writing.

Soon after I heard from other sources that she was married to the regimental sergeant-major of the 1st Europeans. This, of course, settled all my hopes with a vengeance, and I resolutely tried to forget her, though, I am afraid, with but poor success.

I heard no more about her till four years after. I was then with my regiment in front of Gwalior, having in the interval gone through three years of hardships in the shape of marching, fighting, and what not; enough to make me forget there was such a word as love, to say nothing of the object of it. I was sitting in my tent one day when a letter came directed to me in her well-known handwriting. If there is such a thing as knocking one down with a straw, that operation might easily have been performed on me at that moment, for I felt ready to drop. I was afraid to open it in the tent, for I was so overcome with the sight of her handwriting, that I thought I had better go away by myself to read the contents for fear I should betray myself before the men. I, therefore strolled out of camp, and sitting down on a bank, tore open the letter with a beating heart and devoured its contents.

It was written from Roorkee, where the 1st Europeans were stationed, and sketched all that happened from the time I left her. She had but recently discovered that her mother had intercepted all my letters to her, and likewise those written by Rose to me, with the exception of the first one, which, as she knew nothing of it, she could not intercept. The poor girl had consequently arrived at a similar conclusion to mine—that I had forgotten her, or thrown her aside for someone else; she had, therefore, in despair, accepted the first eligible offer, and married the regimental sergeant-major, with whom she led a most wretched life. She wound up with incoherent expressions of unaltered love to me; that she would—regardless of her marriage ties—leave her husband and find her way to me, if I still entertained the same feelings for her, and would receive one so guilty as she.

Here was a pretty fix to be in! I found that I still loved her as much as ever. That letter had stirred up every half-dormant feeling of my heart, and I felt as if we had not been separated a day. But had I wished it ever so, how could she come to me through a country swarming with rebels? Or, if she even succeeded in reaching me, it was not very probable she would be allowed to remain, which would make things ten times more desperate. I, therefore, wrote a hurried reply, that I loved her as dearly as ever, but entreated her, if not for her own, for my sake, to bear as well as she could her present unhappy life, and on no account to leave her husband, or endeavour to join me; explaining, as well as I could, its utter impossibility. I concluded by bidding her hope for happier times, when the war was over, and we were once more in quarters, when, if she still held to her determination, I would gladly receive her, and endeavour by my love to efface all remembrance of her present unhappiness.

I never had another letter from her, from what cause I never could ascertain, and, of course, I could not write for fear of committing her, in case the letter should fall into her husband's hands. A few months after the Mutiny was suppressed we were ordered down to Bombay, and shortly afterwards my regiment was ordered to England, and I accompanied it.

Two years after I arrived home I left the service. One day I accidentally encountered a man who had formerly belonged to the 1st Europeans; on getting into conversation with him, I found out a little more about Rose. It seems her husband led her an awful life, for he was perpetually taunting his wife with her former intimacy with me—some kindly-disposed person having made him acquainted with it probably—or, perhaps, he had become possessed of my letter. Be that as it may, he was constantly taunting her about me. One day he had done so beyond her powers of endurance, when she in her passion suddenly seized a knife and stabbed him. Whether he died from the effects of the wound, or what became of her afterwards, the man could not tell me; for he was on the eve of leaving the regiment when it occurred.

Poor girl! I have never heard a sentence about her from that day to this; but though twenty years have passed since I told her I loved her, I often feel sad even now when I think of her unhappy life and probable fate.

And this tragic termination to our pleasant though stealthy love-making, was brought about through that infernal old Dummy's Hoo-hoo-hoo-oo-oo-o-o!

CHAPTER 11

The March to Kirkee

At this time the British were at war with Russia; and, to our great joy, we were ordered to hold ourselves in readiness to proceed to Bombay tor the purpose of joining the forces in the Crimea, by the overland route.

We hastily disposed of our superfluous kits and the various sundries which had accumulated during our long stay at Meerut—for some of us had enough clothing and other *etceteras* to break the back of an elephant—and reduced them to regimental dimensions.

In a few days the order to march came, and off we started, in high feather at the chance of having a go in, the band of the 81st playing us out of the station; the men of the different regiments stationed at Meerut, no doubt, envying our prospect of soon getting into the thick of honour and glory.

We were not destined to get away so easily, however, for at Hauper, a place where the well-known stud is kept, the second day's march from Meerut, a courier came in, mounted on an express camel[1]; he was the bearer of orders from headquarters for us to return to that station, which we did, to our intense disgust and annoyance.

Having disposed of all the fixings which made the barracks look habitable, we found on our return the rooms empty-looking and desolate; the very appearance of them, together with our disappointment, made us feel anything but cheerful. There was no help for it, however, and we put the best face on the matter we could. Shortly after, owing, I believe, to some representations made to headquarters, we were again ordered off, and this time with better success.

This being my first march with the regiment, everything for the

---

1. Some of these camels are said to travel as much as 350 miles in one day, and to continue this for sereral days in succession.

first few days wore a novel appearance, altogether different from my marching up the country as a recruit. There we had mostly bullock-*hackeries* to carry our tents and baggage; here, we had elephants and camels, and it was astonishing to see how expert the men were in loading them. By-the-bye, I had always heard and read of the patience of the camel, but a more impatient and cantankerous animal I would not wish to see; apparently taking a grim delight in throwing all sorts of obstacles in the way of loading, by snapping at the loaders, or trying to struggle up and shake off its load just at the ticklish moment when the wretch knew the final knot was to be tied, which would render all secure[2]; often succeeding, too, to the annoyance of the men, who would have all the work to do over again, while the offending camel would wobble out his intestines (I always put this down as his peculiar way of expressing his glee), as if he enjoyed the extra trouble he caused them.

I could not but admire the regularity with which a camp was laid out, and the rapidity with which the tents were pitched, causing what had a few minutes before been only a waste bit of ground, or a cornfield, to assume the appearance of a tented city, it being laid out in streets according to the troops. Thus, the regiment consisting of eight troops, there were eight rows of tents; space being left between the rows of tents for the "horse lines," that is, two rows of horses with a pathway between; each row of tents, or troop of men, having two rows of horses; the horses being picketed opposite the tents to which their respective owners or riders belonged.

In the centre of the camp was the main street—a wide space having four troops, with their horse lines on either side. Exactly in front of this street, and at some little distance, was the main-guard tent, and that of the regimental sergeant-major; facing these, at the other or rear-end of the street, was the officers' mess-tent, &c. The officers' tents and hospital tents were in rear of the tents of the men, and behind all was the rear-guard tent. Of the camp-followers, and they were very numerous, some slept in the horse lines, or under the lee of tents, &c., but the greater portion lived a short distance from the camp. There was also a large bazaar with the regiment; its long street of small tents, with the wares of various kinds temptingly displayed in front of each of them, was pitched at a convenient distance, and reminded one

---

2. Long experience had taught the men that, if they wished the baggage to be brought in expeditiously and safely, the best way was to fasten it on securely themselves, repudiating native assistance altogether.

greatly of the stalls in a fair; and it certainly must have been a great convenience, not only to the natives, but to many of the men; for almost anything required by them on the road was to be obtained in the bazaar, and which could not possibly have been got but for it.

We used to start at 2 or 3 o'clock in the morning, according to the length of the march, so as to get to the next camping-ground before the sun was very high. The first blast of the trumpet which roused us was the signal for a general hubbub. In a moment such a din arose as it would be impossible to describe; hundreds of fires were lighted, throwing a lurid glare on all around, in the midst of which were seen tents falling, and men, horses, camels, and elephants apparently in the most inextricable confusion. This was heightened by the shouts of the men, the neighing and snorting of horses, the trumpeting of elephants, the guttural growling of camels, and a hundred other indescribable sounds, making the camp for a time appear a perfect pandemonium.

A very short time, however, sufficed to reduce all this confusion to something like order; the tents were struck and packed, the animals loaded, the horses saddled and bridled, each man standing by the head of his horse, waiting for the sound to mount, when we silently filed out of the lines, "fell in," were "told off," and on the road in no time; seeing, while this went on, strings of loaded elephants and camels noiselessly gliding off into the darkness like so many phantoms. A glance behind, as we were leaving what had been our camp, would show us the fires still burning, with the camp-followers, who had not yet "cleared out," running hither and thither among the fires, and appearing in the distance like so many demons.

It is needless to describe the incidents of the road, or enumerate the places of note we passed, among which may be reckoned the celebrated Taj at Agra, and the fort at Gwalior; suffice it to say that, after a long but pleasant march through all sorts of wild and beautiful scenery, we at length reached Kirkee, a cavalry station about five miles distant from Poona, in the Bombay Presidency.

CHAPTER 12

The Bull Pup

We had no sooner arrived at Kirkee than we received intimation that the orders to proceed to the Crimea were countermanded; so that our long journey counted for nothing more than a shift of quarters, besides knocking up the horses, many of which were condemned as worn out and unfit for service. As soon as possible, therefore, those whose horses were cast were remounted on young horses, the breaking-in of which occupied them fully for some months.

In the meantime, as I always had an eye to all sorts of amusements to beguile our leisure hours, I had not been idle, but had looked out a suitable building for a theatre, and soon transformed it into a very comfortable little place. The finances of the theatrical company being in a somewhat shaky condition, through the mismanagement and extravagance of a former manager, I was elected stage-manager, and empowered by the colonel to do what I thought necessary to get the company out of debt. I was even struck off duty so that I might devote my whole time to this purpose, and I was, after a few months, able to clear off old debts and issue dividends to the members according to their rank, a thing that had never been heard of before among them; so that I got credit, not only as a player and manager, but as a first-class financier. I likewise started dances in the regiment again, and was rewarded by the gratitude of all the women of the regiment—the young ones in particular. These and other amusements caused the time to slip away very pleasantly, in spite of our disappointment about not being sent to the Crimea.

My position as stage-manager, master of the ceremonies, and the being recognised as a bit of a poet as well, made me a great favourite with the girls of the regiment; and, I believe, not one of them would have refused an offer of marriage from me. I am afraid, on looking back after this lapse of time, that I must have been abominably conceited—an egregious fop, and something of a man-flirt as well; but whatever I was, I am bound in honesty not to hide my failings, or make myself appear more virtuous than I really was, and I'll make no attempt at doing so. I, therefore, frankly admit, right or wrong, that I felt not the slightest compunction in writing amatory poetical effusions, or making violent love to half-a-dozen different girls at the same time.

Among the girls of the regiment was one known by the *sobriquet* of the "Bull Pup." I forbear to mention her real name, but many will remember her by that name even now. She could not have been above fifteen, and, although she was remarkably plain—having a round "full moon" face, large mouth, and a snub, or rather *retrousse* nose, which got her the cognomen of the "Bull Pup"—yet she had beautiful hair, bright eyes, a soft voice, and was a well-shaped graceful girl, being withal an excellent singer and dancer. She was, therefore, if you could look over her face, what I should call a nice little lovable girl; somewhat gushing, but that is often pleasant, especially when the gushing has a tendency to flow in your direction. She was, also, a great admirer of my verses, which, perhaps, caused me to feel a greater interest in her than I otherwise should.

I first got into favour with her by soothing her girlish feelings, which had been deeply hurt by being slighted at one of the dances. Her mother—as some mothers absurdly do—indulged the foolish notion of keeping the girl, although she was quite womanly in her development, in clothes ridiculously short; and the girl felt this keenly, the more so because, owing to this, she knew that she was looked upon as a little chit of a girl, while she felt that she was in reality a woman; and this peculiar costume affected her so greatly, that, much as she liked dancing, she could hardly get a partner while any of the more womanly-dressed girls were disengaged.

One night a young sergeant, seeing all the ladies had partners except the "Bull Pup," requested her to "stand up" with him, which, of course, she readily agreed to, especially as he was a good-looking young fellow. He was about to lead her out, when a woman of the regiment whom he knew entered. He, without scruple, at once deliberately left the girl, walked over to the woman, and engaged her instead, leading her off regardless' of what the girl might think of his conduct. This naturally hurt the poor girl's feelings very much, and she sat down, on a seat, pouting, and looking as if she felt very much disposed to have a good cry. Seeing her sit thus, I went to her, and said,

"Have you no partner?"

"No," she replied, half-sobbing; "Sergeant Mayhew *did* engage me, but, seeing Mrs. Eames come in, he left *me* and engaged *her*, because she was a woman, I suppose, and I am only a girl in short dresses."

I at once offered my services, which she gratefully accepted; that is, if I could judge by the look of her eyes. Shortly after, I rebuked the sergeant, in her presence, for his want of politeness, which seemed to gratify her very much, for she looked as if she thought I was quite a champion. My manner towards her gave her such confidence that she did not hesitate to innocently ask me to stand up with her next time, and to always dance with her. I explained the impossibility of doing the latter, but I did dance the next time with her, and several more dances during the evening, and I could plainly see I had quite won the heart of the little "Bull Pup" by my unlooked-for kindness.

Although she was very plain, she had several eligible offers—the particulars of which she used to confide to me, so that I considered myself in the light of her confidential friend and adviser; but she declined them all, perhaps thinking I should eventually propose for her; for we had certainly become very affectionate, she thinking nothing of allowing me to kiss her. She would even steal out of an evening to meet me, and on receipt of a few verses would throw her arms round my neck and outpay them with kisses.

One evening, we had snatched a hurried meeting, and were bidding each other an affectionate farewell—our faces being in unaccountably close proximity—when, through the gloom, we fancied we saw pass the form of one of the rejected suitors of the girl—a, corporal of her own troop. Uncertain whether he had observed us or not, she hastened into her house, and I speedily evaporated in a contrary direction.

In the morning there were floating rumours about that the "Bull Pup" had been seen overnight kissing a man near her house. These rumours in the course of time reached her mother's ears, and she taxed her daughter with the monstrous crime of surreptitiously kissing someone, and insisted on knowing who the individual was. The girl stoutly denied the imputation, protested it was a calumny invented by some evil-disposed person who would probably have liked to have undergone that operation himself; reminding her mother that on the particular evening in question she sat with her sewing and never once quitted her side, so how could it possibly have taken place?

The mother determined to fathom this mystery to the bottom,

so she set to work to find out who first promulgated in the regiment such vile slander concerning her daughter, and after some trouble succeeded in finding out the originator of it, who, proving to be a rejected suitor, she gave him the credit, in her own mind, of circulating the scandal out of revenge. The old lady was in such a way about it that she declared she would horsewhip him herself, and at once proceeded to put her threat into execution. She sought him out and commenced laying into him lustily with the whip, which, of course, the surprised corporal did not submit to long, for he easily took the whip from the enraged mother.

The case was brought before the captain of the troop, and he, hearing the particulars, also concluded that the corporal had spread the report out of malice; he therefore gave him a severe lecturing, and after mildly rebuking the old lady for resorting to violent measures by taking the law into her own hands in vindication of her daughter's character, dismissed the case. The corporal thus got the credit of being a revengeful discarded lover; the mother was held to be one that would "stick up" for her daughter's reputation; and the daughter was esteemed a much maligned and ill-used girl, and gained the sympathy of all the other girls of the regiment.

We had many a laugh afterwards over the adventure, but were very careful to confine the real facts of the case to ourselves, so that they never oozed out. As for the corporal, so much was his conduct reprobated by everyone that in time, I believe, he thought he must have been mistaken, and that he really was the unprincipled and vindictive individual he was currently represented to be.

While I am at it, I may just as well relate another curious incident, which, although it did not take place just in the order I here put it, will not inappropriately close this chapter. I relate it only as showing a queer side of human nature, and that the awful and the comical may be blended together. The reader must not suppose, either, that I was serious in my portion of the incident.

The "Bull Pup" had a married sister much older than herself, with whom I was on very friendly terms, often visiting her at her husband's quarters, and was treated both by herself and her husband with marked kindness.

One day the husband of this sister took it into his head to quit this mortal sphere, leaving his disconsolate widow to mourn his loss. Nearly all the married people and their families attended the funeral, and I, though not married, politely escorted two young ladies of the regiment there, so that I was equivalent to a married man and family.

I must confess I was somewhat shocked at the levity of these girls, for the whole of their conversation, during our progress to the cemetery, and when one ought naturally to have had serious thoughts, was about plays, dances, novels, new dresses, and a variety of other inappropriate funereal topics. This made me begin to think of the widow, and wonder what her ideas on things in general might be; whether she might not at the present moment be revolving all sorts of plans in her own mind as to what she will do now she is again free, and who she has got her eye on for a second. Having a dim recollection that I had heard some peculiar tales of the rapidity with which widows can forget their defunct lords, I determined, if possible, to test this one on the road back from the cemetery, as to the likelihood of her remaining long in that lonely state.

When the funeral obsequies were over, therefore, I gradually edged near to the widow, who was disconsolately looking on whilst the men were filling up the grave; and when the last shovelful of mould was placed on his grave, and she was in the act of tearing herself away from so melancholy a sight, I demurely offered her my arm to conduct her away from the hallowed spot, and take her to her now solitary home. She as demurely took my arm as I had offered it, and we proceeded homewards. Not a word broke the silence for some time, not a sound but her suppressed sobbing, till at last I thought if I wanted to carry out my plan I must commence at once. I, therefore, in a soothing voice, intimated that she should not give way to unavailing grief, but rather think how she might forget her bereavement as soon as possible.

"In fact," I continued, "I sought the opportunity of escorting yon home so that I might speak to you on a subject nearest my heart—to offer my services—a—in endeavouring to soothe your natural grief—and—a—you know—at least, I always fancied you perceived—you must—that I—I—always had a—a—sincere regard for you. Let me then—that is—consider me as your devoted admirer—your lover, and I will hope, eventually, your—a—husband."

"Oh, Mr. ——!" exclaimed she, "I am *so* sorry! Yes, I always did think you a very nice young man. But—Sergeant Wiggins spoke to me on this subject *coming down*, and I have accepted him."

Coming down! Accepted him! This reply knocked me out of time altogether. I thought I was going to be remarkably smart in catching her coming *from* the cemetery; but here was one sharp enough to catch her going *to* the cemetery, propose for her, be accepted, and all this done under the very nose, or rather behind the body, of her defunct husband on his last journey to his final resting place.

The old soldier, when in a moralising mood, would remark, "Women are strange animals." After seeing the widow home, I went off home myself, and moralised in a similar strain.

CHAPTER 13

The Tables Turned

As I mentioned in a previous chapter, I was elected stage-manager of the theatrical corps belonging to the regiment; this election was ratified by the colonel, and I was empowered by him, through the adjutant, to do what I thought necessary to get the company out of debt.

My first proceeding was naturally to curtail the expenses as much as I possibly could; this I did by closely inspecting all bills, and ascertaining whether the articles mentioned in them had been really used or not[1]; never allowing anything to be sent for by the workmen without an order from me; I taking care to know first that they really wanted it, and what they wanted it for. Then I cut off such extravagances as suppers after performances were over, as not being a legitimate way of expending theatrical funds, and tending only to demoralise the members of the company by setting them "on the spree" after each performance, thus getting the body of amateurs a bad name.

By pursuing this system—though at first I incurred a certain amount of odium, as being a bit of a tyrant, and a nip-cheese to boot—in the long run the whole of them found it was for their own good, and as our debt decreased, their dividends and my popularity increased in ratio, till, finally, the wisdom of my proceedings was fully recognised by all hands.

I must here relate a trifling but amusing incident which occurred at the commencement of my reign, to show what opposition—I had almost said mutiny—I had to encounter. Among other expenses incidental to the theatre was that of the band for the orchestra. These

---

1. Under former managements, it was a common thing if a workman wanted a few *rupees*, to go to the purveyor, get the *rupees*, and tell him to put it in the bill as so many yards of cloth, pounds of paint, &c. It is needless to say the shopkeeper did not lose by this, but that we did.

men, numbering about twenty, belonged to the regimental band, and were allowed certain pay and refreshment every night of a performance, whether their services were required to play in a piece or not; and they had a very easy and pleasant time of it, often having nothing to do but look on, consequently they were able to enjoy the performance, with the additional gratification of receiving pay for it as well.

But these men, knowing the difficulties under which I laboured in my efforts to get the company out of debt, and being themselves, at present, the only ones who received payment for their services, fancying—as they could not be dispensed with—any terms they chose to make must necessarily be complied with, demanded an increase of pay; threatening, if their demand was not acceded to, to refuse to play the music required in the pieces; in other words, to strike for higher wages.

Annoyed by their ingratitude and want of consideration. I resolutely refused to give them an increase till such time as we were fairly out of debt. No more was said on the subject; but shortly after, a performance was to take place, in which it was announced I was to sing a comic song between the pieces. I went to the bardmaster, arranged the accompaniment with him, and everything was apparently progressing all right.

However, the day before the play was to take place, one of the bandsmen came and informed me that his comrades intended to spoil my song by playing a wrong accompaniment, which would naturally throw me out, and probably cause me to break down. Thanking the man for his kindness, I immediately made arrangements to neutralise or counteract this conspiracy.

The song I was to sing was "Vilkins and his Dinah"; and I was supposed to carry a clarionet under my arm while singing it. I at once set to work steadily to master the tune on the instrument, which I, after much practice, succeeded in *too-too-ing* off to admiration. Confident now, I did not care what they played, as I could play the air of my song after they had finished whatever they intended playing, and give myself the key-note.

The performance took place the next night; everything went off successfully, till I appeared on the stage to sing my song, when, instead of the band playing "Vilkins and his Dinah," they struck up the "College Hornpipe." I was quite prepared for the occasion, but waited patiently till they had finished, when I publicly reprimanded them for their scandalous behaviour, and told them it was fortunate I was not left entirely at their mercy, for that I could do without their assistance. I, forthwith, too-too-ed the tune out on the clarionet, sang the first verse, and then called on the gallery to join in the chorus; I need not say they cheerfully responded and lustily joined in. I then too-too-ed the air over on the clarionet, repeating the same process at each verse till the finish, when there was a perfect storm of applause, and I had to sing it again; so that the trick the band thought to play me turned out to their discredit and to my triumph.

Some of the officers came behind the scenes to ascertain the cause of such an unwonted proceeding; among the rest was the adjutant, to whom I related the origin of the affair. He was much annoyed at their behaviour, and mentioned it to the colonel, who was also so much disgusted at it, that, when the performance was over, several of the ringleaders found themselves politely escorted to the guard-room.

The next morning they were brought before the colonel soundly rated by him for their conduct, and various terms of "kit-drill" were fairly divided amongst them to teach them better in future. Henceforth, I was ordered never to pay them anything at all, as they were struck off duty expressly to play for the amusement of the regiment. I followed out the colonel's instructions to the letter; their avariciousness thus in the end greatly benefiting the funds of the theatre.

I could here relate many amusing incidents connected with theatricals, but will refrain from doing so, lest the reader should get surfeited with having too much of the subject; I shall, therefore, dismiss that topic, and proceed to jot down scraps of personal adventure, amusing or otherwise, till I can lead him or her on to scenes more in unison with the real life of a soldier in India.

CHAPTER 14

Scratch-Cradle

By way of keeping my mind thoroughly occupied, I must needs get into a "hank" with a girl of the regiment named Annie Holt. I knew I was not really in love with her, but chose to fancy myself so, or, I suppose, the weak points of my nature were flattered up to that pitch by the evident partiality she showed for me, on the principle that love begets love, even if the begotten love is of an inferior quality to that which begets it.

Thinking this a capital way of forgetting Rose, and testing on scientific grounds the advantages to be derived from a counter irritant, after preliminary love-makings, in the shape of squeezes of the hand, sly glances, whispered soft nothings, &c., at the different places in which I met her, I came to the conclusion that I would go to work this time in a legitimate manner; march off to her mother, tell her the state of the case, and request her to allow me to call at the house occasionally, so that I might have better opportunities of seeing and making myself agreeable to the daughter under the mother's own immediate supervision and with her sanction.

All this I thought I could do without actually "popping the question" till I saw how things were situated.

Full of this idea, I crossed over to the *patcherie*[1] one morning, and knocked at the door, *not* with a beating heart, which was a convincing proof in my own mind that I was not *very* far gone in love.

The mother opened the door herself, and without expressing the least surprise, after the usual morning salutations, she said "Come in, I've been expecting for a long time that you would call. Annie has told me all about it."

---

1. Detached bungalows on both flanks of the regiment, where married people resided; each married man with his family occupying a separate bungalow.

Here was a start! I was anticipated; I had been expected! The daughter, like a good girl, had dutifully told her mother "all about it." All the little episodes that had passed between us had already been discussed, much to my regret and annoyance, thereby depriving me of an excellent opportunity of making use of some very flowery language I had composed expressly for the present occasion.

I went into the house, under these altered circumstances, and managed to tell the old lady that I had seen her daughter a good deal latterly, admired her very much, and had reason to believe I was not altogether distasteful to her, that I wished she would allow me to visit her here, so that I might have a better opportunity of cultivating her acquaintance than I could by casually meeting her at parties, and I had too high an opinion of her daughter to attempt to meet her by stealth.

The old lady quite approved of my conduct in coming to her first in such an honourable manner, her daughter—she didn't mind telling me—was a good girl, and had told her she liked me very much, but then, she was young, we were both young, and either or both of us might alter our minds; she, herself, had not the slightest objection—in fact, she thought it a very good match—her daughter would not come empty-handed, but that she must first consult her husband, and would I call again in the evening at 7, when she would let me know the result of her conversation with her husband. She was sure he would have no objection—oh dear no! but then it was only proper to speak to him first. "I shall not let Annie know anything about it till I hear what her father says," continued she, conducting me to the door; "poor girl! she will be delighted, and—good-morning, I shall expect to see you about 7."

Not a bad beginning, I thought, as I wended my way back to my barrack-room. The girl was considered quite a catch in the regiment, her father being orderly-room clerk, and a sergeant-major to boot; the mother was known to be a very careful woman, and it was rumoured that she was in possession of a pretty long stocking. Neither of these things, however, had any influence with me, for I was neither ambitious nor mercenary, and, on the other hand, I thought myself rather an eligible character. I was only a private, to be sure, but then I could have worn the stripes had I chosen; but I was. better off without them, and had declined them, as everyone knew, several times. I was, moreover, young, passably good-looking, to say nothing of my various accomplishments; in fact, any girl of the regiment would have "jumped at me" for a husband.

Annie, on her side, was young, as her mother had truly said, being only fifteen; she was also very good-looking and graceful—I think I had better dispense with any elaborate description of her personal charms, suffice it to say she would pass muster anywhere. The most attractive thing about her was her hair, which curled naturally, the ringlets appearing to be scampering wildly all over her head and chasing each other down her back and shoulders; they were of that peculiar hue that one was in doubt whether to style them "golden" or "carrots." Above all, I had it from her own lips—second-hand, it is true—that she liked me.

I went again to the house in the evening punctually at 7, feeling, I admit, slightly sheepish, but that soon wore off after the father and mother had given the required permission to visit there when I liked, and I soon began to feel myself a little more at home.

Annie, who on my arrival had rushed off to an inner room, was now persuaded to put in an appearance, blushing as red as her hair, yet looking very pretty and very happy, and we all sat down to a very pleasant tea.

After tea, a married couple entered, with the intention of spending the evening there; then came two young girls, companions and bosom-friends of Annie's, and a young widow not yet twenty—not the one I proposed to—who had recently lost her husband, and very becoming and bewitching she looked in her black dress; so that there was quite a large party of us, including Annie's brother—a sort of hobble-de-hoy—whom I omitted to mention before.

The four seniors sat down to a game of whist, and we, the youngsters, including the widow, sat down to "hunt the slipper," "scratch-cradle," and such scientific games, where it was quite the reverse of "whist."

I cannot let this opportunity pass without saying a word or two concerning the interesting game of "scratch-cradle." Language fails in the description of it; it is simply delicious when played by those who are "spooney" on each other—at least, that is my idea of it. It requires such care in taking the string off to prevent its getting tangled. And the tact that is necessary to keep it from slipping over either of the tiny fingers! The perpetual contact of your fingers with hers, to prevent such a catastrophe, or, the catastrophe having occurred, your efforts to place the string back again into its proper position; these, together with the necessity of both leaning over till the two heads come imperceptibly together, and your hair gets entangled with hers, in place of the string—you can't separate till you have carefully taken the string off her fingers, which takes some time—and you feel in such a glow, and so flurried, that you are sure to drop a string, and have to do it all over again, with a similar result. I say that scratch-cradle is positively a delightful pastime, and would become a favourite game with lovers did they but once try it. It is for this purpose only that I mention it, that others, if they wish it, may have the benefit of my experience in this delectable game.

After having indulged in these games for some time, the young widow suggested—it being a clear moonlight night—going out on the grass *plat* in front of the house and playing "Sally Waters," to which everyone, myself included, cordially responded, though I had not then the remotest idea of who or what "Sally Waters" was. We, therefore, went out, and at once commenced this interesting game.

For the information of those readers who have not played it, I will briefly describe it; at the same time admitting, that whatever opinion the reader may form of it, and however absurd and childish the game may appear, there is one point in it that meets with my warmest approval:—I mean the kissing part of the ceremony. This is particularly enjoyable, unless the player is of a misanthropical turn of mind, when, of course, such enjoyment is not to be expected.

One of the players stands in the centre of a ring formed by the others joining their hands together. These, then, commence a sort of war dance round the one in the centre, at the same time chanting—

Sally, Sally Waters,
Sprinkle in the pan.

(I haven't the slightest conception of what they are supposed to "sprinkle in the pan," or what kind of pan it is.)

Arise, Sally Waters,
And choose a young man.
Choose from the east,
Choose from the west.
Choose from the whole of us
Whom you like best.

The central player, designated as Sally Waters, whether male or female, then chooses one of the opposite sex; the two kneel facing each other, and the "war dance" and chanting are continued—

This young couple are married together,

Father and mother they must obey;
Love one another, like sister and brother;
This young couple must kiss each other.

The ceremony of kissing each other having been solemnized, the one who was the first in the centre then quits it and joins the ring of "war-dancers," leaving the one he or she has just selected to remain in the centre and repeat the same performance on someone else, when he or she retires in turn from the centre; this sort of thing being repeated till the players are tired of the game.

I enjoyed this game very much, and was particularly fortunate, I being the only male present, with the exception of the hobble-de-hoy brother, who was out of modesty generally chosen by his sister, after she had been chosen by me; so that I came in for a full share of kissing, hobble-de-hoy never being chosen but by his own sister, the other girls and the widow invariably choosing me, much to my gratification and appreciation of the game.

At 10 it was time for us to disperse to our respective domiciles, and I now found out, for the first time, that Annie went every night to the bungalow of a lady who had recently come out from England (and whose husband was away superintending some railway works), and slept with her, as the lady was rather nervous at being left alone in a strange place. I, of course, offered to escort Annie to the bungalow; the widow exclaiming she would also go with us. So off the three of us started, left Annie at the bungalow, and I came back with the widow alone. On our way back I could plainly see that she was making a regular set at me; I, however, pretended not to perceive her drift—leaving her, perhaps, under the impression that I was rather "slow" and stupid, when in reality I was aware of her purpose and simply fighting shy of her lures.

The widow was young and handsome, in fact she might safely come under the head of "bewitching," but she was, undoubtedly, also, up to a thing or two, and must have been a trifle unscrupulous, for she knew how Annie and I were situated, and yet she very palpably "set her cap" at me. Every evening she found her way to Annie's house, proposed "Sally Waters"—to which, all the others being agreeable, I could not possibly object—and invariably accompanied Annie and myself to the lady's bungalow; by this arrangement depriving me of a *tête-à-tête* with Annie, and securing one for herself when I escorted her back. In short, being familiar with the flavour of her lips, and rather liking it, in "Sally Waters," it came natural to me to take more lengthened draughts from them than the exigencies of the game actually required; on our road home we had also got into the habit of rehearsing that particular part of the game, so that it would appear as if I came to see the widow instead of Annie, when, really, I did not care for the widow—not that I disliked the kissing—but I kissed her for fear she should think I was a fool to throw away, or not avail myself of, such luxuries thus put in my way. I could see the danger I was in—not of being "hooked" by her, but of being eventually found out—such a state of things could not continue long without being discovered, and then there would be a pretty scene.

One night the widow chose me for her "young man," in "Sally Waters," and when we knelt down, and the cue was given to kiss, she said, "Now, give me a nice one." I replied, foolishly, and without giving it a thought, that I would give her the sweetest I had, and kissed her, taking no more notice of it. It was now my turn to select one, and I naturally chose Annie; on taking her hand to kiss her, she slipped a ring I had given her a few days previously into mine. I dropped the ring at once into my coat pocket, as if nothing had happened, and retired from the centre, joining the rest in the "war dance," but, at the same time, I felt uneasy as to why she had returned it to me.

When it came to Annie's turn to quit the centre, she slyly stole away into the house. A few minutes after, watching my opportunity, I followed, and found her in tears, and her mother trying to soothe her. I asked her why she had given me the ring back, and it then all came out:—the widow's nightly propositions for "Sally Waters," her constantly choosing me (I should have thought it strange if she had chosen hobble-de-hoy), and as constantly accompanying ns to the lady's bungalow, and coming back with me alone (fortunately she did not know of our rehearsals on the road); and, to wind up all, the widow's asking me to give her a nice one, and my reply. This was all told with much sobbing and many tears.

In defence, I could but say that I came there to see Annie only; that I did not invite the widow, and did not want her to come, but I was only a guest myself, and could not reasonably tell her she was not wanted; that she did not accompany us at my invitation but her own, but that it was not in my power to drive her away; that if she proposed the game, and the rest all appeared agreeable, it would be very bearish in me to object; as to the words I made use of when she requested me to give her a "nice one," they were said without thought, and I should probably have made the same reply to anyone else under similar circumstances; that if she or her mother liked to prohibit the widow from coming there, it would give great pleasure to me, as I should then be able to enjoy more of Annie's society alone. In short, we made friends again. But the same scenes constantly occurred; the widow still came; Annie was still jealous, and scarcely a night passed that we did not have a squabble, till, finally, a rupture took place and we mutually agreed to separate.

I could not have felt much regret at this, for it did not prey very heavily on my mind, but I also could not resist the temptation of writing a few lines, and sending them the following day to her, to show the effect our separation had on me. Some idea may be formed of the state of my feelings by a perusal of them, I will therefore insert them here; they run thus:—

Rejected! cast off! my love coldly slighted;
For did not her own lips the cruel words say,
That have wrecked all my hopes, and my happiness blighted?
"I don't love you now, though I did t'other day."

"I don't love you now!" those words were too bitter;
I felt the blood rush to my fingers and toes;
Oh! where was my spirit, that I didn't hit her
A "topper for luck" on the bridge of her nose!

Yet I know she once loved me; have not her lips said it?
Has she not told her love by her blushes and sighs?
When her eyes have met mine, have I not in them read it?
And does not the heart speak its love through the eyes?

To that lonely graveyard, by the side of the river,
I'll be borne like a mummy, within the dead cart;
And people will say 'twas complaint of the liver.
But she will well know 'twas disease of the heart.

And women will come, and with tears and with wailing,
Mourn over the grave where my virtues lie hid.
And say, "He'd no fault, he had only a failing;
He didn't love wisely, but too well"—so he did!

There shall I rest, and nought shall awake me.
Till the last jolly trumpeter sounds the "fall in,"
When I'll rise, and an escort of angels shall take me
To where there's no suffering, sorrow, or sin.

We were shortly afterwards ordered off to Persia, so I had no leisure to fret, even if I had the inclination; constant change and excitement effectually prevented my giving way to any serious amount of melancholy; indeed, I looked upon the whole affair as an exquisite joke, and an agreeable way of having passed my time for the last few weeks.

It may be as well to state here that I did not see Annie again till I came back from the Indian Mutiny, nearly four years after; I then heard she was engaged to be married to a corporal of the 6th Inniskillings, and that her *trousseau* was already prepared. I was at this time lance-sergeant, having accepted the stripes when I found we were really going into the field, and had risen to the rank of lance-sergeant in the ordinary run of promotion.

To return to Annie. I met her at a dance one evening, and purposely avoided her, but, to my great surprise, she crossed over, and shook hands with me, during the time we were waiting—both of us being in the one set—for the dancing to commence, and, after a few hurried words of greeting, asked me to stand up in the next dance with her. I could not nicely refuse, so I danced with her in the next, and, in fact, in nearly every other dance afterwards. That night she told me she still loved me, and that she wouldn't marry this corporal. I had great difficulty to check her ebullitions of love, which, although I felt a sort of secret pleasure in, I heartily deplored, as I found I had not the slightest tenderness for her now.

From this evening I avoided her as much as possible, but she took every opportunity of meeting me, and even writing to me, begging me to be again to her as I was before. Hobble-de-hoy, too, who had been with me through the campaign, and who had by this time grown a great strapping fellow, must needs invest in a pistol, for the purpose of polishing me off. His friendly intention he darkly hinted to some of the men, who, in turn, told it to me. He thought better of it afterwards, or found out things were different from what he suspected, I being blameless, and not wanting to run away with his sister. To make short work of it, I was very glad when the regiment went home, taking me with it, and leaving her with her friends in India.

I heard afterwards that her marriage with the corporal never took place, he—fortunately, perhaps, for his peace of mind—"stepping out" with a fever; she married some civilian in Bombay.

CHAPTER 15

Off to Persia—Singing Girls

You may say what you like, but the line of march is the place for genuine enjoyment, that is, if you like open-air exercise at all, and don't want to sit puking in hot musty rooms all your life. Fine, bright, sunny weather, with a dash of coolness run through it, just to make the air bracing and invigorating; good roads; a good horse—not a shuffler, but one that can walk out when required and I'll engage that after a march a good breakfast does not go begging—nor a "snifter," either, previous to paying your devotions to the substantials.

Somehow or other, I always felt a different man altogether when I once got fairly on the road. I was really a soldier then—threw away all my foppery and conceit, and got sunburnt as soon as I possibly could, by rambling to my heart's content all day after I had come in from the march. Many men prefer a nap after their breakfast—indeed, the "nip" they have taken before it predisposes to sleep; but give me a run over the country, the wilder the better, and if I *must* have a nap, let it be under a tree, with the whispering leaves to lull me off to sleep.

Our regiment marched off by troops or squadrons, as the case might be, and as fast as vessels could be fitted up in Bombay for the reception of the horses, leaving a few days' interval between the marching off of each detachment.

I had, shortly before we left for Persia, and after my little *fracas* with Annie, been made a lance-corporal.[1] As I mentioned in the foregoing chapter, I had several times been offered that dignity, but declined, principally on, account of the theatre and other amusements. When the order came for us to proceed to Persia, there was an end to theat-

---

1. For the information of those who do not know the difference between lance and full rank, I may here mention that the former is a sort of brevet rank; the recipient wearing the stripes, holding the rank, and doing the work, but not getting the pay.

ricals at once, and I returned to my duty as a matter of course.

The first guard I mounted, the regimental sergeant-major "fell me out," and I was again offered the "stripes," but, as usual, I respectfully declined them. The sergeant-major, who was a kind man, and evidently wished to be a friend to me, pointed out the folly of my declining rank, and the ultimate benefit that might accrue to me by accepting it—that we were now going on a campaign where promotion might be very rapid—that I was a smart man, and ought to aspire to something better than the *rôle* of a private—with other persuasions of a like nature—till I told him I would accept it. The same day my name appeared in regimental orders as lance-corporal, to do duty in K troop; I was relieved off guard, and was soon accommodated with gold *chevrons*, shoulder-knots, &c., the insignia of my exalted rank.

I may as well here mention that it was considered a great mark of favour to be promoted in the manner I was, for everyone aspiring to the rank of lance-corporal had, after receiving a hint on the subject, to write an *application* to become one. I was exempted from this operation, and was, therefore, the more satisfied with my position on account of the omission, as no one could say I had *asked* for rank, or "crawled" to my superiors in any manner.

It soon came to the turn of my troop (the K) to start, and off we went as light-hearted as possible. Some of the married folk—the women especially—pulled very long faces, though perhaps the husbands, if the truth were told, did not object to a little outing by way of a change. If so, they didn't let on about it in presence of their better halves, looking as glum and demure as if they were going to a funeral, instead of on a campaign; but I noticed in a day or two they bore the separation like men, and rather cheerful ones too in many cases—at any rate, separation didn't appear to affect their appetites.

The road from Kirkee to Oolwa, whither we were to proceed in order to embark the horses in native boats, in which they were to be conveyed to the ship, is very pleasantly diversified by plain, mountain, valley, and *topes* of mango trees, while here and there were rugged old forts in the distance, perched on the top of apparently impregnable rocks, looking down on the cornfields and mango *topes*, guarding them and the owners of them who dwelt in the little villages nestling at their feet.

In this short march from Kirkee to Oolwa we had an advantage over our previous marches,—we did not require tents, which saved much time and trouble; for, instead of having to pitch tents at the end of a day's march,, we simply picketed our horses and walked into a Pendall, and on leaving, *vice versa.*

After breakfast I used to issue forth for a ramble; and, so long as I knew I was not required, even when on duty as orderly corporal. At the top of the Khandalla Ghauts one day, knowing nothing particular wag required of me till dinner time, I went out for my customary stroll. Seeing a fine tope of mango trees a short distance off, I sauntered in that direction and sat beneath the luxuriant foliage of one of them. Chancing to throw my eyes up in the tree, I noticed a very peculiar-shaped bough,, which, by some freak of nature, interlaced with another, and formed a sort of armchair. Thinking what a cosy place that would be for a nap, I climbed the tree, seated myself in this natural armchair, and, dreamily watching the dancing lights and shadows caused by the sun and breeze on the foliage, and listening to the whispered rustling of the leaves, I insensibly dropped off to sleep.

I was awakened by the tinkling of a *sitar,* and the voice of a woman singing an Indian song just beneath me under the tree On looking down, I saw two Indian girls, one of whom was singing to the accompaniment of a man who played the *sitar.* Still keeping my perch in the tree, I lazily listened to the singing of the girl, till, by chance, knowing the song she was singing, I noticed she missed a verse, and at once betrayed my whereabouts by calling her attention to the omission, and, to the intense surprise of herself and her companion, singing the verse for her.[2]

This put me on good terms with them in a moment, and I was soon out of the tree sitting among them, chatting and singing with them as if I had known them all my life, and was brought up like them to vagabondizing about the country and singing for my living. The girls were tumblers as well as singers, and exhibited before me, but they were perfectly astonished when they found I was equally as well up in that as I was in singing, going through a variety of acrobatic performances for their delectation, and concluding by strolling round in an inverted position, *i.e.* on my hands.

Shortly after, seeing by the sun that it was nearly dinner time, I

---

2. The reader must not put this down as gasconading, for *then* I would not turn my back on any Indian singer, in regard either to the singing or the number of songs I knew. I am now quite an old man and have forgotten a good many, but I could still manage to sing a number of Indian songs, even after this lapse of time. I need not say that the learning of these songs involved a good deal of time and trouble, and led me into some very queer company; and sometimes into rather awkward adventures—my teachers being invariably Indians of the softer sex.

took leave of my quondam friends and walked back to the Pendall. In a few minutes I was in uniform, had donned my belt, and was again on duty, "all there," serving out the beer to the men and looking after their *khana*. After I had finished and reported "all right" to the sergeant-major, he called me on one side, as if he had something particular to tell me, and said, "Are you the orderly corporal today?" I gave him to understand that I had the honour of being that responsible functionary.

"I thought so," replied he, "when I saw you so busily occupied under those trees a short time ago; but I never knew till now that it was part of the duty of an orderly corporal to do the amiable to singing girls, or to walk about on his hands instead of his feet; I find, however, that I was mistaken, and it is so."

It seems he had been watching me from the Pendall, and, with the aid of his telescope, had seen my performances in the acrobatic line, and was, I have no doubt, much instructed and amused by them. Often, after that, if he had occasion to tell me to go anywhere, he would say quietly, after the order was given, "You may go in the usual way; you need not fatigue yourself by walking on your hands,"

CHAPTER 16

Monkeys

We halted for a day at the Khandalla Ghauts, and the next morning I took the opportunity for a ramble down some of the *kudds*. I think there are not many places with such wild and magnificent scenery as is to be seen at the *ghauts*. One could stand on the top of these and behold the mountains stretching far away into space in an infinity of forms, weird-like and grand, as if at the creation of the world they had been tumbled out there promiscuously. On looking down, one could see the village at the foot of the *ghauts*, and fancy it was the simplest thing in the world to toss a stone into it, when in reality it is seven or eight miles distant by the winding and picturesque road.[1]

But to return to the *kudds*. I had gone down a very steep one, sometimes at the risk of breaking my neck, greatly admiring the scenes that occasionally opened out to my view, and the nearer glimpses of grotesque-looking rocks, and numberless unknown (to me) flowers and trees, that I passed on my way down. On reaching the bottom, which seemed as if it was shut out of the world altogether, it was so awfully silent, I found a spring rippling over some rocks and falling into a natural tank or basin, which looked to me as if it was expressly designed for a bath. Under this impression, and being tired and hot, I thought I might just as well freshen myself by treating it as one. I, therefore, peeled off, and was soon luxuriating in its cool limpid water; letting the tiny stream from above make a waterfall over my head, and dash from thence into the basin in which I was comfortably seated, in

---

1. Since I was there—indeed, the work was going on before I left India—engineering energy and skill have triumphed over nature, and, what with tunnelling, bridging, and blasting, an apparently impossible feat has become an established fact, and a railway now traverses the *ghauts*; no doubt astonishing my friends the monkeys, and other wild denizens of these *kudds*, and causing them to remove farther from, the rumble of the train and the shrieks of the engine.

the same costume in which Adam is supposed to have been dressed before Eve discovered the impropriety of his appearing in that style before her.

After indulging in the bath till I considered myself sufficiently cooled, I got out, dressed myself—without the aid of either towel, comb, or glass—sat down on the edge of the basin, lighted my pipe, and proceeded to placidly enjoy a smoke, listening meanwhile delightedly to the musical trickle of the water as it fell into the basin.

On all sides of me rose precipitous rocks, with here and there a wild flower or stunted tree sticking out of their very faces, though how a seed could ever find its way to such a place—how flowers and trees could find root-hold, to say nothing of the moisture requisite to cause them to grow—but there they were, and growing as freely as if they were carefully tended and watered every morning.

While revolving this phenomenon over in my mind, I was all at once roused from my reverie by an unearthly sort of "cackle"—for I can describe it by no other word—and on looking up to where the sound proceeded from, there was an old "jocko" high up on the face of one of the rocks, making faces at me and indulging in his "cackle"—in surprise, I suppose, at seeing me there.

After watching him for a few minutes, I picked up a stone and threw it at him. This had an *un*desired effect. Little did I dream of the result, or I would not have thrown that stone. The enraged jocko made a peculiar noise, and in a moment the faces of the rocks in every direction were swarming alive with monkeys. Where they could all spring from so rapidly passed my comprehension altogether. The first monkey seemed to explain something to them, when all of them immediately commenced gesticulating violently, gibbering, cackling, making the most hideous grimaces at me, and pelting me—or rather throwing bits of rock or stones at me, fortunately without hitting me. I began to feel uneasy; there were enough of them to eat twenty men, with their clothes to boot, so that I should have been but a mouthful apiece, had they attacked me—and, by their threatening manner, it appeared as if they intended to do so.

Dim visions of being made a meal of by monkeys, and of my carefully picked bones lying in this horrible *kudd* for years, passed across my mind. When I was missed I should have the credit of having been eaten by tigers—they would never think of monkeys eating me. Would they, search for me when I was missed at the Pendall—if they did, would they find me? The monkeys wouldn't eat my *chuckmuck* and pipe, I should be recognised by them. In fact, the near prospect of being "skoffed" by the infuriated monkeys was sufficiently alarming. Here was a pretty finish to all my capers! What a nice thing to put on my tombstone—if ever I had one—"*Eaten by monkeys!*"

I was getting afraid—in fact, there is no use in mincing the matter—I *was* most decidedly afraid, and would, have turned tail and run away if I could, but the infernal place was so steep, I should have all my work to do to get out of it at anytime, without having an army of chattering monkeys at my heels. It ran through my mind, too, that if I once turned my back and fairly fled it would only encourage them; I should have the whole boiling of them on the top of me in no time. I *must* get away, however, that was evident; so I slowly retired, in great trepidation at the necessity of proceeding so slowly, showing a front as much and as often as the nature of the ground I had to pass would allow; but it seemed an awful long journey to the top of the *kudd*. I reached it at last; followed to the very top by the whole of the monkeys—who must have numbered thousands, and who mouthed, chattered, grinned, threatened, and pelted me the whole way. I was very thankful when I once more put my foot out of their realm, and considered myself safe. I did not go down that *kudd* again, and I inwardly resolved never to pelt a solitary monkey, if I saw one, no matter where he was.

Lest the reader should imagine this monkey adventure a little overstrained, I need but mention that among Hindoos, in all parts of India, monkeys are held in great veneration, many temples being dedicated to Hanuman, the Monkey God, who figures largely in Hindoo mythology. I remember reading once that this worthy, who was a great warrior, sent out 350,000,000 of monkey generals to reconnoitre; and I thought at the time, if so many generals went out to reconnoitre only, how many monkey generals and soldiers must there have been when it came to actual fighting. Monkey temples, therefore, often contain numbers of real monkeys, as well as the effigy of Hanuman. Pugger Tank, the only one I can call to mind by name, having some thousands, I should think, running about the premises, and fed by the establishment.

There are many temples, also, where such "cattle" as lice, fleas, &c. are fed and housed very comfortably by the priests, who take great care that they are properly looked after in regard to their diet. For instance, in the rooms where these vermin are kept, is a great quantity of clothing and bedding which literally swarm with them. At feeding-time, which is at night, a number of beggars are turned into the rooms, their own clothes having previously, been taken away from them; they are required to don some of the clothing belonging to the temple, containing the vermin, or sleep, if they can, on the beds .provided for them, while the vermin browse off them (the beggars) to their hearts' content. In the morning the beggars receive a few *pice* as remuneration for their night's rest (?). Their clothes are restored to them, and they are allowed to depart, leaving the vermin no doubt greatly refreshed with their feed, and looking forward to night again, when another relay of beggars will be found to replace those who left in the morning; thus insuring the vermin a change in their diet, as they never feed off the same joints two nights consecutively. But I am digressing, perhaps, led to it by the affinity between monkeys and vermin; they (the monkeys) enjoying nothing better than a *battue* on a brother monkey's head to search for and kill the same creatures that their human brethren philanthropically endeavour to preserve and fatten.

I must not omit to mention that while on this march I also climbed up to the Karlee caves, and was amply rewarded for my labour in the magnificent view which greeted my eyes on attaining the summit of the rock in whose bosom the cave is situated. I was much impressed with its grandeur, and the immense amount of time and labour that must have been spent in its excavation, and in the grotesque carving with which the cave is ornamented. It has been too often described by tourists and others better qualified than myself to explain its various beauties to need a feebler repetition of them at my hands, I shall, therefore, refrain from inflicting a description of my own on the reader, and content myself with remarking that the place is well worthy a visit.

On this rock, too, I saw a very peculiar sort of tree, the leaves of which are of a beautiful mauve colour, transparent, like stained glass; while the blossoms, also transparent, were a brilliant green. I am not much of a botanist in regard to a knowledge of the scientific names of flowers, plants, or trees, but I have a keen appreciation of their beauty, and I could not enough admire such a singular and beautiful tree; it put me in mind of the trees one reads of in fairytales. It is the only tree of the kind I have ever seen, and could it be transported to England would cause somewhat of a sensation among those who make botany their study. It is a pity some effort is not made to propagate the tree by cuttings or seed, if it has any, and I trust my casual remarks may induce some lover of the beautiful in nature to at least make the attempt to do so.

At Oolwa the horses were put into native boats, each boat having its complement of *ghora-wallahs* to look after the horses, and one dragoon to look after *ghora-wallahs*; the remainder of the men and the camp-followers embarked in the governor's yacht, the name of which I forget. As we slowly steamed away, there arose from the little landing place such a plaintive wail from the poor Indian women who crowded there to get a last look at their husbands, fathers, brothers, or lovers (I mean English lovers), that I felt quite sad for the poor creatures, more so than I had recently felt when leaving our own women at Kirkee, and I was thankful that I had left no one to wail for me among the crowd, or I might have felt sadder still. Even when out of ear-shot of their cries, we could see them wringing their hands and gesticulating for a long time, and I was glad when distance and the increasing gloom shut them out from our sight.

The next morning we reached Bombay, and went on board the good ship *Tornado*, the vessel "told off" to take my troop to Persia. In a few hours the horses were all safely shipped, stowed away in their stalls below; and off we started, with a fair breeze, for Persia.

CHAPTER 17

On Board Ship

Not being much of a politician, I had not the remotest idea of the origin of the Persian War, nor, I must confess, have I up to the present time. Nor did I care either; it was sufficient for me—and the rest of us, so far as that goes—that there was to be war, and that we were ordered to Persia to participate in it, which was satisfactory for all parties, blind obedience being one of the first qualities of a good soldier.

Now I always endeavour to make myself at home whereever I go—as was the case with the singing girls; and in this particular instance, having landed on board ship, as Pat would say, I was at once eminently nautical. I went to my pack and drew out a seafaring rig I had previously prepared, which I donned in a brace of shakes, substituting a rakish-looking wide-awake for my shako, a striped shirt well open in the neck and displaying a reasonable amount of breast for my full-dress coat, a black neckerchief loosely tied with a slip-knot, and the two ends flying loose for my stock, a pair of white ducks, tight from the waist to my knees, and from thence gradually widening to the bottom, where they were as wide as pyjamas, for my overalls; as for a substitute for boots and spurs, I scorned a covering of any kind for my feet, and went barefoot. A clasp-knife suspended by a string from my neck, and stuck in the waist of my ducks, supplied the place of my sword and completed my outfit.

In this costume I considered myself pretty well "got up" as a tar, and that I was complete in everything, except a knowledge of sailor's work. This, however, caused me no concern; and I very soon set to work to rectify that by learning the names of the ropes; sails, &c., and I made no scruple in going up aloft to help reef or stow sails when it came on to blow. Whether I was ever of any assistance at such times was best known to the sailors, but on after-consideration I am inclined to the mortifying belief that I was no great help, but rather in the way occasionally; I did not, however, perceive this at the time.

But to proceed. I had scarcely rigged myself out and stowed my regimentals away when the trumpet sounded for the guard. I stood aghast at the sound. Here was a devil of a start! I was orderly corporal, and it was my duty to parade the men, inspect them, and report to the sergeant-major previous to his and the captain's inspection. But what a costume I was in to inspect the guard, who were in "full uniform." It was no earthly use asking one of the other corporals to do it for me, as they were all in a similar predicament to myself, they having already mounted slop clothing, but having the advantage of me in wearing shoes.

Seeing I had no alternative I determined to "cheek it" out; so I put on a hold face, and gracefully standing with one hand on my hip, in approved nautical fashion, I roared out, "Fall in the guard!" and stood, barefoot as I was, ready to parade them. The men assembled, looking rather surprised at me and my costume; and the vision of the captain standing on the poop with his glass stuck in his eye, staring very intently at me, as if I was some queer description of animal he had never seen before, alone deterred them from bursting into a roar of laughter. I need not say that I was very far from laughing at the time, but I determined to carry it off in the best manner I could, so I bawled out the words of command, as if, instead of being barefoot, I was in full dress and on a general parade.

"Ten *shun!*"

"Eyes *right!*"

"Dress!" (I wished I had been properly dressed at the time.)

"Up a little on the left!"

"Steady!"

"Eyes *front!*"

"Port *arms!*"

"As you were!" (I'd have given a trifle to have been as I was previous to putting on this infernal rig.)

"Together; port *arms!*"

"Half-cock *arms!*"

Having given these necessary words of command, I commenced making a careful survey of the men, slowly walking down the rank, looking them up and down—while they as intently stared at the front busily occupied in looking at nothing—taking a bird's eye view down the nipples of the carbines, to see if they were properly cleaned, straightening a belt, &c. When I arrived at the bottom of the line, I gave the words, "Ease springs! Advance arms!" and then inspected them minutely in the rear. This being done, I bawled out, "Stand at ease!" and, the sergeant-major having in the meantime put in an appearance, I went up to him with the greatest nonchalance, as if I was doing the thing in the proper regimental style, and reported "All right."

I could see a merry twinkle in the sergeant-major's eye as I approached him. But, the captain being on the poop at the time, he was compelled for his own sake to notice such an absurd breach of discipline as a barefooted corporal inspecting a guard in full-dress. "All right, except you, I suppose you mean," cried he, addressing me sternly. "What do you mean by such a masquerading costume as that? Consider yourself under arrest." On this, of course, I *did* consider myself in that unpleasant position, and immediately hid my diminished head by dropping into the background.

Shortly after I was "had up" in front of the captain, who, after closely scrutinising me and my "get up" through his eye-glass, demanded to know what I meant by such conduct. I excused myself on the plea that I had entirely forgotten that I was orderly corporal, or rather that I did not think that on board ship the guard would mount as they did on shore, and had changed my costume, as I thought, to suit the place I was now in, and the sort of work I might have to assist in doing.

The captain, merely remarking that he had no objection to the sort of clothes I wore on board ship—here I detected his eye-glass unconsciously straying to my feet—but that I ought to have waited till I was off duty, released me. The men afterwards mounted guard in slops, indeed, constantly wore them; but I, unless on duty, always stuck to my nautical costume.

CHAPTER 18

Incidents at Sea

I do not know a cooler or pleasanter place in a ship, when at sea in the tropics, than the fore-top. You are, as it were, like Mahomet's coffin, between heaven and earth—or, rather, the deck of the ship—with the breeze, if there is one, all around you, wafted towards you in its proper course, bounding down on to you from the bellying fore-topsail, coming up to you through the battens on which you lie. With your head pillowed on the slack of the fore-topmast staysail, you may sleep as serenely and coolly as if angels made it their business to exercise their wings for your express behoof. Even if there is no breeze at all, the flapping of the sail against the mast answers all the purposes of an immense fan, and soon sends you into the regions of oblivion.

I used to spend most of my leisure time up there—and I had a reasonable amount of that, for soldiers are not overworked on board ship—and pass the hours very pleasantly, either in a game of chess with a comrade—and we had some great chess-players in the regiment—reading a book, or dreamily staring up through the maze of ropes and sails, into the bright blue sky, till somnolency, in it sweetest and most seductive form, insensibly stole over me. Yes; the fore-top of a ship is the place, *par excellence*, for either dreamers when awake or sleepers whether dreaming or otherwise.

I was once reported absent from a parade, and much uneasiness was felt lest I had mysteriously fallen overboard, till one of the men, knowing my proclivities, suggested the fore-top, where I was discovered, fastly locked in the arms of the drowsy god, to the great relief of my comrades.

Another favourite place of mine was the extreme end of the bowsprit. On a breezy, sunny day, with a good sea on, it was delicious to stand or sit there, and, according to the motion of the vessel, be one moment lifted high up into the air, the next plunged down again as the good ship dipped her nose into the briny,—as if she intended diving under it altogether,—shook herself, and again bounded on.

I remember once being there when the stentorian voice of the boatswain hailed me with, "Come in out of that; do you want to make us have to stop to pick you up?" I came in as desired; but, my pride being touched by an allusion the boatswain made to "land-lubbers" and "horsemen," what should they know about ships? I challenged him, and offered to bet my porter against his grog, that, "land-lubber and horseman" as I was, I could do on the bowsprit what he couldn't. The bet was accepted at once; I immediately went out to my old position, and, supporting myself with one hand by the "royal stay," and with the other by the end of the bow-sprit, stood on my head, and, while in that position, making an excellent figure-head of myself, calling on him to come out and do the same, if he could. I need not say he did not come; the laugh was turned against him for being beaten by a land-lubber, and he owned I had fairly won his grog. He never called me in again, nor a land-lubber either.

As I did not at the commencement of this history inflict on my readers a diary of the "passage out," I may be pardoned for narrating an incident here, which occurred during that period. About 8 o'clock one evening we were spanking along with a fair breeze, at the rate of eight or nine knots an hour: at the same time many of the men and women were also "spanking along" through the mazes of country dance, to the inspiriting strains of a fiddle, fife, and tambourine, when all hands were startled by the cry "A man overboard!" This cry did not proceed from anyone on board, but from someone in the sea at the stern of the ship.

There was something awful in this, and some of the women fainted. In a moment all was confusion. "Who could it be?" "How did he get there?" No one on board had seen or heard anyone fall in, yet there was the cry from the water. Another faint cry, apparently a long distance astern, came borne on the breeze to our horror-struck ears. It was too dark to see anything, but the captain promptly ordered silence, hove the ship to, threw out life-buoys, and had a boat lowered, which proceeded in search of the man. We were in a dreadful state of anxiety to know who the man was, though there was not much hope of the unfortunate wretch being saved, whoever he might be; for there was a heavy sea running, the night was intensely dark, and he must by this time have drifted a long way astern.

This suspense lasted for half an hour, which to us seemed an age, till at last we heard a welcome shout front the distance which informed us it was "all right!" After what appeared a tremendous long time, the boat came alongside, and the man stepped on board as naked as he was born, and to all appearance perfectly unconcerned at the narrow escape he had just had. He was found by the crew of the boat sent to search for him clinging to one of the buoys, and had given up all hope of being rescued from his perilous position. A cloak was thrown over him to spare the blushes of the ladies, and he was taken below by the doctor; a dram of grog was prescribed and taken, and in a short time the man presented himself on deck as if nothing had happened.

On inquiry, it was elicited from him, that, seeing all hands enjoying themselves at dancing, he thought that would be a capital opportunity for a bath; he, therefore, went down the fore-chains, stripped himself, and, after making fast a rope to one of the chains, he lowered himself into the sea. He contented himself for a short time by holding on to the rope with one hand and swimming with the other; at length, knowing himself to be a good swimmer, he thought he could safely let go the rope, swim by the side of it, and resume it again when he felt tired. He, accordingly, let go his hold, but had scarcely done so when he found himself rapidly drifting astern, and in a moment was in the wake of the ship, from whence he had raised the cry, "A man overboard!" which had put so abrupt a stop to our dancing, and alarmed us so much.

Another curious incident took place on the same vessel, but of a more laughable kind. One of the men, an Irishman, had fallen backwards from the deck into the lower hold; we naturally expected, from the distance he had fallen, to discover that he had broken some of his limbs, if not his neck. What was our surprise to see him briskly jump up, shake himself, and, instead of ascertaining whether he was hurt or not, as we had anticipated, hastily clap his hand on his pocket and exclaim ruefully, "Be jabers! if me dudheen isn't all into smithereens!" His pipe being the most important consideration to him from the fact of its being "beautifully coloured," *i.e.* beastly black.

One of our recruits on the passage out to the regiment had a narrow escape from death, under such singular circumstances that I will briefly relate it, though it does not properly belong to this narrative. This lad and another had a bit of a fall out, and determined to settle it in the orthodox manner, that is, have "three rounds "and done with it. They at once peeled off and commenced operations, when the steamer giving a lurch—there being a good deal of sea on at the time—one of the combatants rolled over to leeward into the sea. Every effort was immediately made to save him, but by the time the boat was lowered he was some distance off, and could only occasionally be seen, owing to the heavy sea, and it was a long time before the boat succeeded in reaching him.

Fortunately he was an excellent swimmer, or he never could have been saved; for, independent of the risk he ran of drowning, he had to defend himself from the attacks of a huge albatross which kept swooping down at him; so that the poor devil had all his work to do to keep afloat and intact at the same time. I have often heard him describe the adventure, and the dread he felt lest the bird should scalp him or tear his eyes out before help could reach him, for on each attack of the bird he could see his eyes evidently gloating over his anticipated prey. The bird missed a dinner, however, on that occasion. After a good deal of hard pulling, the boat managed to reach the lad, and brought him safely on board, none the worse for his dip and his fight with the albatross. It is but right to state that the combatants, from that day to this, never finished the orthodox "three rounds."

As I am now in "full swing" relating board-of-ship anecdotes, and as I am not going to write a description of my voyage home, I will, with the reader's permission, introduce another incident, of an awful nature, which occurred on our way to England.

One of the men of my troop had been washing his clothes privately, it not being "washing day," and was hanging them out to dry on the bowsprit stays. We were going through the water at the rate of seven or eight knots an hour; the wind being fair aft the jibs could not fill, and consequently kept flapping to and fro.

The man was sitting or stooping on the stays, tying his clothes to them, when one of the ropes belonging to a jib or a block—it was not perceived which—knocked him into the sea. A boat was lowered at once, and life-buoys thrown out. The captain hove the ship to, and called out for one of the soldiers to run up to the mizen-top—the jailors being busied in lowering the boat and attending to the necessary work required in heaving the vessel to—to see where the man was. I instantly ran up, but was scarcely there when I heard such an awful scream that it made my very blood run cold, and the sound of which I did not forget for a long time.

I anxiously looked astern for some sign of the poor fellow, and perceived his cap at some distance off. I called out to the men in the boat, and they rowed in the direction of the cap, which they picked up, but nobody was to be seen, though the men asserted that the water was tinged with blood. The man, when he gave that appalling scream, must have been seized by a shark and devoured in a moment; for on the boat's reaching the ship's side—after rowing for some time in the neighbourhood of the cap, in the vain hope of yet seeing him—an immense shark actually tried to jump into the boat to get at the men, which frightened them so much that they nastily clambered up the side of the ship for fear he should succeed in his daring attempt.

A hook was, immediately baited with a large piece of salt pork, which the voracious monster swallowed almost as soon as it was low-ered down into the water, and he was at once hooked. Unfortunately, on pulling the brute up the ship's side, and when we fancied we had safely got him, the hook broke, and the shark escaped, so that we lost the only opportunity of knowing if he had really devoured our unfor-tunate comrade, or not; we, however, gave him the credit of it, and to judge by his size—for I should think he was fifteen or sixteen feet in length—he could easily have devoured one man, and, by his voracity in trying to get at the other men, he could readily have found room for one or two more in his capacious maw.

This incident cast a gloom over all on board, more especially those of his own troop, who knew that he had been saving his money for years, with the intention of buying his discharge, taking a small farm, and supporting his widowed mother. How true is the French say-ing *Homme propose, Dieu dispose*. Who would have thought that all his hopes of home would be thus cruelly and abruptly terminated? I often used to wonder what the feelings of his poor mother must have been when she heard the sad news of his awful death.

I have seen death in all its forms, and have myself killed, in various ways, more than I can at the present time count; but I never felt so deeply impressed in my life as I did at the death of my troop-mate, poor Bill Trueman; and even now, whenever I think of it, I feel strong-ly tempted to breathe the prayer of an Irish Catholic; that I know, and say with him, devoutly, "God keep us from a sudden and unprovided death."

CHAPTER 19

"Juggler"

Writing the previous chapter has given me a slight touch of the blues, so, to dissipate them, I think I'll change the subject for something of a more enlivening nature. I'll therefore retrace my steps—on paper—to where I ought not to have strayed from—to the gallant vessel (though why they should call a vessel gallant I never could conceive) bearing us to Persia.

The poor horses must have had a sweltering time of it below—they were literally stewing during the whole passage; for they occupied the lower deck, and a hundred or so of horses in the 'tween decks of a ship would make the place feel warm in the coolest of weather, so what must it have been in warm weather in the tropics! They were almost constantly steaming with perspiration, and must have felt the heat very much.

Their stalls—I was nearly writing cabins—were fitted up with every regard to their comfort, and padded carefully to prevent them from getting chafed or bruised by the motion of the vessel. Nets, filled with hay, were hung before each of them, so that they could nibble away at pleasure. They were regularly cleaned, fed, and watered every day, the same as on shore; and would, therefore, have been very comfortable were it not for the intense heat. As for us, we took the decks for it, day or night, and the camp-followers stowed themselves whereever they could find an empty spot to lie down in, or a hole to crawl into.

We certainly had the advantage of the horses in one respect, for if there was a breeze "knocking about" we got the benefit of it; we could lie down too, packed very close, it is true, and pretty moist of a morning when we woke up, from the heavy dews that fell during the night; generally having to wring out our clothes and bedding, and dry them in the sun preparatory to another saturation at night. Fortunately there was no rain, or we should have been in a pretty plight. This was our case; the horses, though housed properly, were stewed and condemned to a standing position for the voyage, much as some of them might have wished to lie down.

Several of the horses succumbed to the extreme heat below; these were dragged to the hatchway, hoisted up on deck, and tossed overboard. One felt a pang at seeing a noble animal surrounded in a moment by a swarm of sharks, who would be seen tearing the poor trooper to pieces, and fighting amongst themselves for the last piece, till he was devoured. After finishing their banquet the sharks would follow the ship hungrily, waiting for another windfall of the like description—they, probably, not being able to get horse for dinner every day of their lives.

One morning a horse was brought to the main hatchway in a dying state, as well to enable the poor beast to get a breath of fresh air from the windsail, as to enable the farrier to see what was the matter with him, and to administer any remedy he might consider beneficial. I happened to be standing by at the time, as were also some of the ship's crew, who used to like to go below and look at the horses, much in the same manner as we should look at the wild beasts in a menagerie; for they did not often have an opportunity of seeing horses, never having occasion to use them on board ship, and horses not being much in their line, so that the sight of a cargo of dragoons with their horses was quite a novelty to them.

While standing thus, in a group round the hatchway, I could hear the sailors wondering among themselves what was the matter with the horse in question. At length, one of them, edging up to me, commenced making inquiries on the subject, the remainder of them preparing themselves to listen to the dialogue, which began thus:

"I say, shipmate, what's the matter with that 'ere horse?"

"Why, the farrier says he is in a consumption," I replied.

Here was a queer start! A horse in a consumption! The sailors looked surprised and solemn at the announcement, while the spokesman continued:

"A consumption! What, do you mean to say that horses get the consumption the same as us" (meaning human beings)?

"Of course they do," I replied; "why shouldn't they? They are flesh and blood the same as we are, ain't they? They get the same diseases too, and are treated in the same manner as we are."

This was an unanswerable argument.

"But," inquired he, "how do you know when they are ill, and what's the matter with 'em?"

"One way is by feeling their pulse, another—"

"Belay a minute, shipmate," exclaimed the spokesman, interrupting me, "till I overhaul the first part. Where is their pulse?"

"Why, in the off hind-leg, of course," replied I, with profound gravity.

Nothing would do but that I must give them a practical illustration, and show them how to feel a horse's pulse; so I placed two fingers just above the hock of the dying animal, and shaking my head, gravely remarked, "that his pulse was very feeble, and that he couldn't possibly hold out much longer."

The sailors all looked very serious at this announcement, which they received as if they were standing round the deathbed of a friend. I continued:

"There are many ways of finding out when a horse is ill, without his actually mentioning it himself" (here the men began to open their eyes and mouths a bit); "though it is much better if the horse does so, for he can describe the symptoms, and the veterinary surgeon has greater confidence in prescribing for the case than if he were left to his own resources in finding them out."

"Why, you speak as if the horses could talk, with your 'mentioning' and 'describe the symptoms,'" exclaimed one of the men, while the rest all stood aghast at the idea of such an unheard-of thing as a horse talking.

"So they can, and do," I replied, "though there are not many persons who understand them; but all veterinary surgeons—unfortunately, there are none on board—must have a certificate of proficiency in the language of horses. I know a few words myself, and if you come with me I'll soon prove to you that horses can not only talk, but that they have got plenty to say for themselves too."

Saying this, I led the way to the stall where my own horse stood, the sailors closely following in my wake, anxious to witness a conversation between a man and a horse. My horse was busily employed in munching his hay when I came up, so I opened the conversation as follows:

"Well, Juggler, how are you getting on this morning?"

"Ha! ha! ha! a-a-a-a-a," replied the horse.

"The deuce you are!" I exclaimed, as if he told me he was unwell, "you seemed to be enjoying your hay well enough when I came up."

"Ha! ha! ha! a–a–a–a–a–a–a!"

"Yes, it is pretty hot down here," I replied (interpreting his neigh as if he had complained of the heat); "but in a few days we shall reach Persia, and then it will all be over."

"Ha! ha! ha! ha! a–a–a–a!"

"Why, you see, it would be rather awkward to shift you now"—as if he had applied to be placed nearer the hatchway for the sake of the air—"and the other horses would think it unfair," I replied.

"Ha! ha! ha! a–a–a–a–a!"

"Yes, you must 'grin and bear it,'" I exclaimed, as if he had re-marked he supposed he would have to put up with it.

"Ha! ha! ha! a–a–a–a!"

"Oh! these are some of the crew who wished to hear you and I have a chat, as they would not believe horses could talk": as if he had inquired, "What are all these fellows doing here?"

"Ha! ha! ha! a–a–a–a–a!"

"No, no, I can't tell them that, it wouldn't be polite, you know"; as if he had requested me to tell them they were confounded fools, and knew nothing whatever about horses.

I continued this farce for some time longer, asking and answering all sorts of questions (translating the neighs of the horse to suit my own purpose), to the astonishment of the sailors, who tried to make the horse speak to them as he had to me, but the horse refused to hold any communication with them whatever.

These men told others of the crew about the conversational pow-ers of horses in general—my horse in particular—and I often had a similar kind of chat with him for their edification and wonderment. The readiness of the horse to talk to me, and to me only, may be easily explained. I had a habit, every time I went to the "lines," of carrying a few cakes, or a piece of bread in my pocket; this I used to dole out to him piece by piece, talking to him as mothers do to children, or as dragoons will talk to their horses—he would naturally, every time I opened my mouth, whinny or neigh for more, till in the course of time he would do so each time I spoke, whether I gave him anything or not—hence the deception so easily practised on the unsuspicious sailors. The particulars oozed out soon after,. and the sailors looked somewhat sheepish when they found they had been sold so readily; and if any of them were at anytime "drawing the long bow" in spin-ning a yarn, they were often "brought to" by the proposal, "Let's go down below and have a chat with the horses!"

Poor Juggler afterwards received a shot in the chest, and fell in one of the charges at the battle of the Betwa!

CHAPTER 20

Sunday Morning

They that go down to the sea in ships, that do business in great waters;
These see the works of the Lord, and his wonders in the deep.
For he commandeth, and raiseth the stormy wind, which lifieth up the waves thereof.
They mount up to the heaven, they go down again to the depths: their soul is melted because of trouble.
They reel to and fro, and stagger like a drunken man, and are at their wit's end.
Then they cry unto the Lord in their trouble, and he bringeth them out of their distresses.
He maketh the storm a calm, so that the waves thereof are still.
Then are they glad because they be quiet; so he bringeth them unto their desired haven.

Never had I felt the full force and beauty of the Psalmist's words so much as I did on this Sunday morning. As the captain of my troop slowly and impressively read these beautiful verses, I felt that the writer of them must indeed have been inspired, or how could he have expressed himself in such exquisite yet appropriate language, which would lead one to imagine he was familiar with storms at sea and the incidents of a seafaring life, when it is probable he was never on board a vessel in his life? I think many of the men felt as I did on that morning, as we stood there bare-headed, reverently listening to and, I trust, joining in "Divine Service."

We had, in the earlier part of the morning, been caught in a cyclone, which seemed to me to have blown from all sides at once. We had been whirled about on the waves as if a mighty ship was but a mere plaything to the mightier wind. We had literally experienced all that the Psalmist had so graphically described; consequently,, having so recently seen "*His wonders in the deep*," we could the better appreciate the truthfulness of the language; and we, I trust, all felt an emotion of gratitude and thankfulness to *Him* who had "*made the storm a calm*."

The service proceeded; the voice of the captain alone being heard in the ship, as she noiselessly ploughed her way over the billows.

How the snowy crests of the blue waves gleamed and glistened in the bright rays of the morning sun as they danced merrily along, as if they were chasing each other in the joyousness of uncontrolled freedom! What a glorious church was ours! On all sides there was blue and white and gold. Above us the blue sky, with "*the glory in the centre*," for our roof; beneath us and around us the blue water, its white-crested waves as they successively curled over breaking into myriads of flakes of foam which, goldened and rainbow-tinted by the glowing rays of the sun, looked like jewels, forming a brilliant moving flooring of beautiful mosaic work; the boundless horizon being the walls of the edifice. Truly a worthy church in which to hold "Divine Service"! And how softly and melodiously our choir, the seething water and the sighing breeze, seemed to murmur the responses on that bright Sunday morning.

Shortly after the service was finished, a steamer was sighted making towards us; as she was coming from Persia we were all on the tip-toe of expectation to get the last news from the seat of war. We were too soon made acquainted with it; for in a short time they neared us, and, to our great disgust, made signals that the war was over and that she had orders to turn back any vessel containing troops that she met. Here, then, was our fiat to return to India, leaving us about as wise as we were when we started.

This news was very annoying to all of us, as we had looked forward to "seeing a little service." We now discovered that five of our troops *had* seen "a little service," for they had been in action. My old troop (the H) had also been up the Euphrates; so that my promotion, having caused me to be removed to another troop, had lost me the chance of being with them.

These five troops had all, fortunately for them, embarked on board steamers, and were consequently not only the first that left India, but the first by a long way to arrive in Persia, the sailing vessels never reaching it at all. I say fortunately, for, although the whole of the regiment started, only those who reached Persia in time to be present at an engagement received a medal; so that five troops had a medal, and the remaining three went back minus the pleasure of a "go in" and the possession of the coveted distinction.[1]

But to proceed. Our vessel was put about, not by very willing hands on the part of the troop, you may be sure, and in a few days after we reached Bombay. We had no sooner arrived when we heard of the Mutiny having broken out, and rumours of the frightful atrocities which had already been perpetrated. We should have something to do after all; and, perhaps, we, who were late in getting to Persia, or rather in not getting there, would be first in the field to help avenge our slaughtered countrywomen. There was some satisfaction in this thought, after our recent disappointment. We were at once transhipped to native boats, forwarded on to Polwa, disembarked the horses and men there, and the nest morning started on the road back to Kirkee, there to await further instructions.

How slowly the time seemed to pass till the other troops gradually came in, and the whole of the regiment had arrived at Kirkee. Five troops were immediately detailed to proceed to Aurungabad to render assistance in quelling the mutiny which had broken out among the; troops of the Hyderabad Contingent, my troop happily forming one of the five. As it was anticipated, we might have some rough work to do before we came back, the authorities sensibly permitted us to wear our turbans instead of the awkward shakos; for which we felt very thankful, the *puggrie*[2] having been our head-dress ever since the regiment had been in India, on all occasions, except when in full-dress, when we wore the shako; now the latter was to be discarded altogether. We also discontinued wearing stocks and gloves; two things that help to make one appear smart on parade, but which, cannot be considered of much service when it comes to actual fighting, especially in an Indian climate. We, therefore, for fear of future accidents, in the shape of being ordered to wear them again, played football for a short time with the shakos, and threw both stocks and gloves away as useless and only so much superfluous baggage.

---

1. I have seen soldiers who served in the Crimea, with no less than four medals, but who have confessed to me that they were never actually "under fire." In India things are different; I have there seen men who have marched more than a thousand miles through the burning sun, have been within sound of the guns, but, owing to being on baggage-guard or other duties, have not been actually engaged, and they have not received a medal. The men used to pass their comments very freely on these facts, not always of a flattering nature to those who manage these affairs.

2. I believe the 14th was the only regiment in India who wore the *puggrie*, till the Mutiny broke out. On account of this we were always styled by the natives the *Puggrie Wallahs* (turbaned men)..

We marched out of the station a morning or two after, burning for the time to come when we could show some good account with our swords on the mutinous Pandys, the men of the three troops that were left behind watching us depart with envious eyes at our being selected to start before them, and longing for the time when they would be ordered to join us.

CHAPTER 21

Aurungabad—My First Charge

At Ahmednugger we were joined by Captain Woollcombe's battery of European horse artillery and the 24th Bombay Native Infantry. There were unpleasant rumours floating about concerning this regiment—that the men were insolent, ready for an outbreak, and refused to march unless served out with ball ammunition, which had hitherto been withheld from them from the dread, perhaps, of what might take place in the event of their proving disloyal.[1]

Whether there was any truth, or not, in these rumours we—the troops—had no means of ascertaining; but, true or not, I know we looked on them with a great deal of suspicion, and, in our own minds, were fully convinced that *they* would be about the first batch of Pandys we should have occasion to practise our swords upon.

It is a very unpleasant feeling to suspect the loyalty of those of your own side—to dread that, at some critical moment, the ones you naturally look to for help should turn round on you. This was our feeling at that time; but I am happy to say we were mistaken, for they proved loyal under all circumstances during the whole of the campaign which followed.

We had just filed into camp, dismounted and picketed our horses, one morning after a long march, and were waiting for the tents to come up, when news came that a portion of the Hyderabad Contingent stationed at Aurungabad—a day's march from where we were—were in open mutiny, and, unless haste was made to succour the few Europeans at that place, and quell the outbreak, there was no telling what the result would be.

---

1. The reader will please bear in mind that I speak only of the impressions the men entertained; these, no doubt, did the 24th injustice, as subsequent events appeared to prove.

We were immediately ordered to get ready for the road again, so, giving the horses their feeds and snatching a hasty breakfast ourselves in the meantime, off we started once more, forgetting our fatigue in the anxiety to be at work amongst the mutineers.

It was about 10 o'clock when we neared Aurungabad. As we came into the station we were met by some officers of the Contingent. Captain Abbot, the commanding officer of the 1st Cavalry, conducted the force to the lines of the malcontents—his own regiment—leaving a squadron of ours and two guns to guard the bridge leading to them; this was done to keep the infantry and artillery of the Contingent in check, in case they rose with the intention of assisting the mutineers of the 1st Cavalry.

On arriving at the camp we were formed up—14th on the left, guns in the centre, and the native infantry on the right. The 1st Cavalry were then ordered to fall in on foot, facing us, which they did, the native officers only being mounted. They were then ordered to give up their arms, and the loyal troopers were directed to fall out and come on our side; some few did, but the majority refused either to give up their arms or come over. It seemed to us that there was too much talking going on, and reasoning with the mutineers; we could also see some of them fiercely gesticulating, and hear them too. Now, instead of smashing in at these insolent fellows and polishing them off as he ought to have done, and which would have saved endless trouble. General Woodburn was foolish enough to give them six minutes to "consider over it"; and, while we were burning to get at them, and the guns, previously loaded with canister, were pointed at them, and could have swept them off the face of the earth, they sensibly availed themselves of the six minutes, so liberally given, to mount their horses under our very noses and escape, we helplessly looking on during the whole proceeding.

The six minutes having expired, the guns were allowed to be fired, knocking over a few picketed horses and a stray *ghora-walla* or two. We, also, were now permitted to charge the empty lines; for by this time most of the troopers, well mounted as they were on fresh horses,[2] had disappeared in all directions; we succeeded, however, in cutting down a few of them, where, but for the absurd six minutes' law given by the old lady of a general commanding, every man of them would have been accounted for.

---

2. It must be borne in mind that our horses had marched forty miles that morning, and that they were naturally pretty nearly knocked up.

We came back from our charge as black as sweeps, heartily cursing the stupidity, or tender-heartedness, of the old general. I am happy to say that the native infantry stood firm, though many of us had thrown uneasy glances in their direction till the affair was settled.

During the day a great many of the mutineers were brought in; some of them were shot by us, the 14th—I trying my hand once or twice myself at potting them—some were blown away from guns or hung; many were flogged, or punished in other ways, and numbers of them were disbanded and turned out of the station, to give them an opportunity of exciting the troops in other stations who had not yet mutinied, but who were quite ready at a moment's notice to do so.

Most of the force shortly after proceeded to Jaulna, to scour the country and to give confidence to the loyal inhabitants, leaving my troop, numbering about seventy men, to guard the station, we being left in a bungalow fortified with a prickly-pear hedge running round the compound.

I have, in the foregoing, given only my own meagre description of the affair; the following extract of a letter written by a gentleman attached to General Woodburn's staff, will give a better idea of the affair than I, with my limited opportunities of seeing or knowing, could possibly acquire:—

A fine sight—14th Dragoons first, then the General and his staff, then the 28th Native Infantry, and Captain Woollcombe's battery last; the rear brought up by a pontoon train, some twenty elephants, and the baggage, extending some two miles in length. We came on to Jobra, and here my mission ended, as the troops were now out of my district, and, indeed, out of the Company's territory altogether; so I went to the General for orders. Mayne had not arrived; and as no one present knew the load to Aurungabad except myself, the General asked me to go on with them, which I was glad to do, as there were worse accounts from Captain Abbot. During the day the General received another express from Abbot, which made him determine to get on by forced marches.

We got into Aurungabad at 10 a.m., and Abbot and his officers came out to meet us. Mayne had joined us just before. It was, fortunately, a cool morning, or man and horse would never have got through the work cut out for them. Well, Abbot told us that things were in a most unsatisfactory and critical state; that since the ladies had left, the officers had lived barricaded in the mess-room; and that there was reason to fear not only the staunchness of the cavalry, but of the infantry and artillery also. He said that we were quite unexpected, and that the best thing would be to march up to the cavalry intrenchments at once and surprise them. The General consented to do so at last. We found some good camping-ground for the force on the Nuggur side of the cantonments, and we inarched on towards the mutineer's lines (1st Cavalry pickets).

Two guns and a squadron of the dragoons were left to guard the bridge, in case of a rising of the Nizam's artillery or infantry; and we went on up to the cavalry lines, which we reached at 12. A long line of white tents, with horses picketed in front, showed us where they were; and the General galloped over the ground to select a good position. All the officers were, of course, with their regiments, so that on the General's staff were only his aid-de-camp (Macdonald), Deputy Adjutant-General Coley, Mayne, Abbot, and myself. The cavalry bugles were sounded, and men ordered to fall-in on foot, except their mounted (native) officers. Abbot then rode past them, and ordered the few men who had remained faithful to fall out of the ranks, leaving the mutineers in a body in front of their lines.

The guns of Woollcombe's battery were then ordered to be loaded with canister, and drawn up within thirty yards; and the General, with Abbot and the other four of us, rode up to the ranks. Abbot was then ordered to speak to the men, and he did so, asking them the reason for disobeying orders, and for mutinying, reminding them that Government never dreamt of attempting to make them change their religion, and of the punishment which awaited them. The mounted officer (a *jemadar*) who commanded this troop, and who was one of the principal instigators of the affair, here broke out: 'It is not good; it is all false' Abbot drew his pistol, and would have shot him as he stood (for speaking in the ranks is equivalent to open mutiny), but the General turned to him and said, 'Captain Abbot, I desire that you will not fire on your own men.' So Abbot put up his pistol, and went on with his harangue.

After another minute the *jemadar* broke out again, 'It is not true; it is all false! Brothers all, prime and fire!' Upon this, with a crash, out came all their pistols; and, had they fired, we six must have fallen, as we were not five yards from them. My pistol, a revolver, was in my hand in a moment; and, as I was next to the *jemadar*, I feel confident I could have shot him before he had time to raise his. But a panic seized them, and they bolted towards their lines, and we rode back behind the guns. Woollcombe had dismounted, and was pointing a gun at them himself; the port-fire was lighted, and one word only was wanted to blow every soul of them to the four winds, and thus strike a decisive and terrible blow, which would never have been forgotten; but the word was not given.

The General allowed them to get to their horses; and then, as they stood in a group mounting, some 260 yards off, Woollcombe ran to another gun, aimed and pointed it, and, losing his patience at not being ordered to fire, sung out, 'May I fire, sir?' If any answer was returned, certainly no order was given; and the rascals got to their horses, and were up and on them and away in a moment. Then came the order to fire, just as they were getting under cover of some buildings; some twenty-nine shots were fired at them, but without effect, only killing some few horses and a poor *ghora-walla*.

The dragoons were then ordered to charge, as the mutineers had by this time cleared their lines, and were drawn up in a line on a plain to our right, out of shot of the guns. Forward went the 14th at a gallop; and the men of the 1st waited in line till the 14th were tolerably near them, and then broke up, and each man turned his horse's head and dispersed in every possible direction. The dragoons caught and cut down some half-a-dozen, and the rest got away.

Towards the evening, nearly seventy of those who had escaped were taken or given up; and this reduced the number of those who had actually got away to about fifty- five. The *jemadar* who had first drawn his pistol was missing altogether, and no tidings could be got of him, though the General was most anxious to secure him. Had the guns opened upon the rascals directly they drew their firearms, not one could have escaped; and a blow direct and decisive would have been struck, and the mutiny in all probability quelled, in these parts, at all events. All were disappointed at the result, and particularly as the General had them so entirely at his mercy.

CHAPTER 22

Harini

The troops started on their expedition, and left us to hold a sort of check over Aurungabad till reinforcements came preparatory to a move up the country on a larger scale.

This was not by any means a pleasant position, cooped up in a bungalow whose only fortification consisted of a prickly-pear hedge, in the neighbourhood of a large city well-known to be swarming with disaffected or disbanded troops and *budmashes*, who, after the recent terrible examples shown to some of their numbers, could not reasonably be supposed to be very friendly to us *Feringees*.

Aurungabad is essentially a Mussulman city, second only to Hyderabad, the capital of the country, which is called a Mahomedan state, that is, governed by a Mahomedan prince, styled a *Nawab* (though the. majority of the inhabitants are Hindoo), in contradistinction to those states which are governed by Hindoo or Maratha potentates.

It was a "native state," or one not directly under the control of the British, except in so far as having a Resident staying at the capital, and of being compelled by treaty to equip and arm a certain number of troops, commanded and officered by British officers. These were called contingent troops; and, on emergency, were liable to be called on by the British Government to serve; but, on the contrary, we had to turn out against some of them, as the foregoing chapter has shown.

The city of Aurungabad, as near as I could guess,, would probably contain about 200,000 inhabitants; these,, not having had many opportunities of cultivating the acquaintance of *Kafirs* and *Feringees*, naturally looked upon us as intruders.

The same narrow, dirty streets and bazaars, that one sees in every native city, were to be seen in this one. It contains the ruins of Aurungzebe's beautiful palace and gardens; and it also possesses a magnificent building called the Fakir's Tomb, which appeared to me to be a facsimile of the Taj at Agra, but that this (the Fakir's Tomb) was *chunam*, while the Taj is of white marble.

I used nearly every day to ramble into the city, regardless of the prohibition to go there, or the scowling looks of the inhabitants. Perhaps, I put a good deal of faith in my knowledge of the language, and the facility with which I could pass myself off as a Mussulman; for, if asked, I used generally to do so, palming myself off as a veritable *hajee*, who had made his pilgrimage to the tomb of the Prophet, and was entitled to wear the green turban. This would invariably cause me to be treated with marked respect; for, in addition to being able to speak the language tolerably well, I could read and write it with ease.

While strolling through the city one day, I was attracted by a pair of the most lustrous black eyes I had ever beheld; not your great staring black ones like beads or doll's eyes, with no expression in them whatever, but eyes of such dazzling brightness, such a liquid depth, such ravishing sweetness, so soft and winning, yet withal so wicked, that I was thoroughly captivated by them. Those eyes were owned by a little Mussulmani damsel, whose face I could not properly see, as she modestly concealed the lower part by drawing a portion of her veil over it with one of the smallest of hands, dimpled like a baby's. She wore trousers, which, being drawn close to the ankle, disclosed the tiniest of stockingless feet thrust into pretty little embroidered *papooshes*.

But those eyes, go where I would,—and I was irresistibly compelled to follow her—were perpetually meeting- mine. I followed her about till she proceeded homewards, and I saw her safe in what I concluded to be her house, which was a large one with the usual amount of dead walls and small loop-holes, with which the houses of wealthy Mussulmans are distinguished. I lingered about the house, hoping to catch another glance of her through the loop-holes; but, not being rewarded with one, I returned home to the bungalow, only to dream of bright eyes, small hands, bare feet, loop-holes, and *budmashes*.

The next day, haunted by the recollection of yesterday's vision, I went into the city again. Instead of rebels and *budmashes*, it might have been swarming with incarnate fiends, and I would still have gone. What did I care for *budmashes*, or any other *mashes*, so long as I could only see those eyes again! I saw her soon after, accompanied by her old *duenna*, and I went through yesterday's programme: following her about, meeting her eyes occasionally, and seeing her home; but rewarded this time by a wave of her little hand through one of the loop-holes.

This sort of thing continued for some time, I becoming more and more infatuated every day; so much so, that I composed poetical effusions by the yard, which I used to put into the best Hindustani I could muster. Some idea may be formed of how far I was gone by the following specimen, which I named "Wants and Wishes." The reader is earnestly requested not to laugh, for I can assure him or her that I was perfectly serious at the time. As far as I remember, some of the verses ran thus:—

Oh! for a small white hand to press,
And that dear hand be thine!
To feel an answering caress,
Whene'er that hand touched mine.

Oh! for those black and lustrous eyes.
Brighter than stars above!
To see them speak their words, their sighs;
For eyes can speak of love.

That last idea I thought a masterpiece. But I will not inflict the whole of the seventy-three verses on the reader; suffice it to say they were all in a similar strain to the two preceding verses, and concluded with the following:—

But what I want most is the heart;
Yes, 'tis for that I pine.
Give me the whole—nay, but a part.
And all the rest are mine.

How avaricious! When I look back on this production,, it seems to me as if I must have been somewhat of a cannibal, and was trying to get hold of a tit-bit, preferring the heart, of course, to any part of the human frame.

She used now, I could see, to come out expressly to meet me, and would smile when she saw me, letting me see it, too, by *coquettishly* dropping her veil from the lower part of her face; and I even succeeded in putting some of my Hinidustani effusions into her hand, which she had tact enough to receive without attracting the attention of the duenna—though after-reflection convinced me that the old lady thought it advisable *not* to see such trifles.

One afternoon, after following her to her home, I was gratified to see her hand appear through the loop-hole as usual; but, after waving it, apparently to attract my attention, she closed it, again opened it as before, and then pointed downwards to a little door in the dead wall. This operation she repeated three times, as if to impress it on my mind. I interpreted these signals to mean, "Be at the little gate at 10 o'clock tonight," and went home fully convinced in my own mind that I had translated them properly; and equally determined to be there, in spite of orders, *budmashes*, or the devil himself.

Accordingly, after watch-setting, I put on a civilian's overcoat I had; took my hare sword-blade, which I concealed under it, with the hilt in my hand, and went to the sentry on the main-gate, who readily passed me out—in fact, being a bit of a favourite with the men. I don't think a man of the troop would have refused me egress or ingress at any hour, in spite of orders to the contrary; for they knew, whatever little *peccadilloes* I might be engaged in, I was always sober; and if it came to anything in the shape of blows, I had all my wits about me, and was well able to take care of myself. Simply remarking, "Hallo! What's your game tonight?" he allowed me to pass out.

On my way to the city I weighed the probable danger I might plunge myself into—(for, take it how I would, I *knew* it to be dangerous)—against the bright eyes of my *inamorata*; and truth compels me to admit that the latter triumphed, as they ought to, of course. However, should anything happen, I had my sword-blade; I could use it too; and I thought, as I went along, that half-a-dozen *budmashes* would not stop me from getting to that little gate in the wall. By heavens! I believe if fifty were in the way I should have a go in at them!

Nothing of the sort took place. I safely threaded the dark narrow streets without meeting a soul, till I came to the little door. By this time it must have been about ten; so, after waiting in the shadow of the wall for a few minutes, I gently pushed the door; it was open, and I hastily ensconced myself inside. I had hardly done so, when I felt my sleeve pulled by someone; it was a little girl, who intimated by signs that I was to follow her. Grasping my sword with my right hand, and my left being held by the little girl, I was led through several dark passages and up a flight of steps, till we came to a sort of hall or lobby. A small lamp, in a niche in the wall, showed some curtains on the left-hand side of the landing. These my little guide drew aside, and disclosed a gloomy looking room—at least as far as light was concerned, for when we entered I could feel there was carpeting on the floor.

The little girl signed for me to remain there, while she went into an inner room, which was also screened off by curtains. I could hear a sort of suppressed shuffle—if the reader knows what that is—and in a few moments the little girl reappeared at the opening of the curtains, and beckoned me in.

My heart beat audibly as I entered the room occupied by *her*. I should at length see her, and be able to tell her—*Kafir* as I was—in her own language how I loved her; how her bright eyes had enslaved me; how—psha!—I entered. There she sat on some cushions, in a sort of recess. I knew it was her, though I could not see her face, which was hidden by her two little hands. I instinctively dropped my sword-blade, which I had carefully treasured up till this, and, throwing myself on the cushions beside her, I poured out a perfect torrent of inco-herent language, in which the words *dil, pyar, pyara*, &c. were largely employed.

I had previously conned over in my own mind some high-flown oriental figures, which I fancied I could use to great advantage, such as some of the beautiful verses of the Persian poet Hafiz:—

Jab se lagi teri ankiyan,
Dil ho gea diwani;
Tn Leila hain, main Mujnoo;
Tu Shera hain, main Kujnoo;
Tu gul hain, main bulbul;
Tu shêmsh, main pnrwana.

Since I felt the influence of thine eyes,
My heart has become mad;
Thou art Leila, I am Mujnoo;
Thou art Shera, I am Kujnoo;
Thou art the rose, I am the nightingale;
Thou art the lamp, I am the moth.

Pooh! What was Leila? A regular old hag, by the side of *my* little Leila, or whatever her name was! Who was Shera? A perfect *harridan*, that would bear no comparison with my Shera! As for Mujnoo and Kujnoo they were milk-and-water characters, who were perpetually whining about love, but never had the courage to tell the objects of it to their faces that they loved; bleating their love to strangers, and keeping those who ought to have known it, in ignorance.

In short, I found my own natural way of expressing myself in Hin-dustani, incoherent though it might have been, was thoroughly appre-ciated. I question if many Moslem young ladies had ever had a lover so energetic in language, or action either; for, on perceiving, after all my rhapsody, she still concealed her face in her hands, I concluded the best way would be to attack any undefended place with kisses, the best weapon I could think of; this would naturally draw the hands to that point to protect it, which would as naturally leave some other place exposed.

This was really delightful occupation, and exhibited a great knowledge of attack and defence on both sides, and I indulged in it with great zest, murmuring, as I attacked each undefended spot, some such word as *pyara* or *dil-khoosh*, till, happening to raise my eyes, I saw my little guide, and another little girl I had not observed before, staring on and contemplating this scene with evident gusto. "*Pyara*" I exclaimed, on perceiving it, "look at those two little girls; are you not afraid they will betray us?"

"Fear not," said the girl, "they are mutes; they cannot, even if they wished."

These were the first words she had spoken, and certainly her voice did not belie her eyes, for it was as sweet as they were bright. Bulbuls are generally put down as having the sweetest voices *par excellence*; but I maintain that the notes of a bulbul would bear no more comparison to the voice of my little one, than would the scream of a pea-fowl with the whooping-cough to the mellow notes of a bulbul.

The circumstance of the mutes having caused her to open her lips, we now began to converse a little, and by degrees I gathered all the particulars of *her* version of our acquaintance, from the day she first saw me till the present time; and I frankly own, that when, on my pressing her, she hid her darling head in my bosom, and whispered that she loved me, I did feel immeasurably delighted; for it is a delightful thing to be told one; is loved, especially when the dear one who tells you so has a handsome form, bright eyes, winning voice, and all the accessions which enhance the value of such a confession. "Oh! if there is a paradise on earth, it is this! it is this!" Those who put that sentence up in the hall of the palace at Delhi could not have been good Mussulmans, for they evidently forgot the *houris* who form the greatest attraction of a Mahomedan paradise.

Each night found me in the *boudoir* of my little *houri*, the fair *Harini* (Fawn); for this I found to be her name, and a charming one I thought it, too, and very applicable, both as regarded her eyes and her fawn-like ways. I made great friends, too, with the little mutes by my kind manner to them; they were not in the least afraid of the savage *Kafir*. Well might they be called mutes; for the poor little things had had their tongues cut out in infancy, and they could not *tell* anything, as my *Harini* had truly said.

I had often heard or read of mutes, but I had never before had an opportunity of seeing them; it not being a general thing for an Englishman to be doing the amiable in a seraglio. I must remark here, that, during the whole of my visits, I never once saw the old *duenna* who had formerly accompanied *Harini* to the bazaar, nor did I feel sufficient interest to inquire; suffice it, that I nightly indulged in my terrestrial paradise, and the more I saw of the little *Harini*, the more I felicitated myself on my acquisition, and became charmed with her. As for the danger of going there, I had utterly forgotten all about it; or was, perhaps, rather reckless concerning it, though I still carried my trusty sword-blade.

One night I was proceeding as usual to the residence of my *Dulcinea*, and was within some two or three hundred yards of the place, when, passing down a narrow lane, I was stopped by a woman, who, in the most earnest manner, begged me not to go to the place where I went every night, as a party of *budmashes* were lurking in the neighbourhood with the intention of murdering me. This intelligence somewhat startled me, but I still felt inclined to proceed, and, in a tone of bravado, showing her my sword-blade, exclaimed, "What do I care for *budmashes*, while I have this?"

"Ah, *Sahib!*" said the woman, "what would be the use of your sword against a dozen *tulwars*? You have been watched coming here every night, and you would only recklessly throw your life away if you attempt to proceed. For *Allah's* sake, turn back while there is yet time."

I was not so foolish as not to perceive that my best course was to take her advice, which I did, with great reluctance; first offering the woman a *rupee* for her kindness in giving me this information, without which I should probably have "lost the number of my mess," and this valuable work would never have seen the light. The *rupee* she peremptorily refused, affirming that she did not tell me for gain, but to save my life. Grateful to her for her kindness, and wishing her to have some *souvenir* of my gratitude, I gave her a kiss, which she unresistingly accepted. I then, with a heavy heart, turned on my heel, and, as the Yankees say, "commenced making tracks" for home.

Here was a dilemma! My nightly assignations were evidently known; and by those, too, who would scruple at nothing to stop them. I could see no reason to doubt the story of the woman; in fact, the kindness she had shown to me, a stranger and a *Kafir*, elicited my warmest gratitude, and I felt convinced she had told the truth. At any rate *she* knew, and, if she did, what was to prevent others from being as well informed as she was? How about Harini? If our meetings were known, what had happened, or *would* happen, to her? My mind gloomily ran through long *vistas* of bow-stringing, tying in sacks, and throwing in rivers, which I had often heard as being the fate of delinquents in *harems*. "Good heavens! perhaps she has already met her death!" I inwardly ejaculated.

I was indulging in these gloomy meditations as I slowly plodded on my way back, when I fancied I heard the light patter of footsteps at some distance behind me. I turned my head and strained my eyes in that direction, but the night was so intensely dark that I could scarcely see a yard off. Perhaps it was the woman following to see me safe out of the city; perhaps one of those infernal *budmashes* stealing after me, in hopes of getting an opportunity of giving me a quiet stab in the back. I was determined to see, so I went first up one street and down another, through several that did not actually lead me straight home but tended in that direction, the same pattering steps still following me.

This convinced me that the steps I heard were not those of a common wayfarer, for a casual passenger could not possibly want to wander up and down the identical streets that I did; it must be someone dogging me. I resolved at least to see who the individual was who so pertinaciously followed me; waiting, therefore, till I came to the next street corner, I turned it sharply, suddenly stopped, and drew myself up close to the wall, ready for a spring on whoever it might be. The person came to the corner, and was in the act of turning it when I dashed out, had his throat comfortably in my left hand, and my sword at his ribs in a moment. The fellow seemed panic-struck, and before he could recover his fright I had taken one of those long curved daggers from his waist and shied it over the wall of a neighbouring house.

This all passed in much less time than I have taken to write it. I again grabbed him by the throat, and seriously contemplated inserting an inch or two of steel between his ribs; fortunately, as it turned out, I did not, but, releasing his throat a little, I inquired what he was following me about for. The fellow seemed too much frightened to give me any coherent replies; so, giving him a farewell shake, I again proceeded on my way homewards.

It must have been getting on for 12 when I approached the bungalow; when within about a hundred yards distance from it, the sentry loudly challenged, "Who comes there?" to which I promptly answered, "A friend!" and confidently advanced in his direction. As I drew near, I could see the white *portico* looming through the darkness, but could not perceive the sentry, as it was so pitchy black. On arriving at the *portico*, out stepped the sergeant-major and the sergeant of the guard.

"Who's that?" quoth the sergeant-major.

"It's me, corporal," replied I, somewhat taken aback at being caught.

"What are you doing out at this time of night?" asked he.

"Oh! a bit of a stroll," I replied, in an off-handed nonchalant manner, though I began to perceive I was getting into it very perceptibly.

Turning to the sergeant, he ordered him to take me to the guard-tent to see what state I was in (*i.e.* drunk or sober). Of course, I knew I was perfectly sober, so I was safe as far as that went; but I had, unfortunately, the sword-blade with me, which was rather a serious affair, persons not being allowed to wander out at night with naked sword-blades instead of walking-sticks. However, neither of them had yet observed it, and I had hopes of their not having the opportunity of doing so, as I intended to rid myself of it as soon as possible. When I entered the guard-tent, therefore, I quietly dropped the sword-blade behind the wall of it, unobserved, as I thought, by the sergeant, and looked at one of the men as much as to say, "Take care of it for me," which I knew he would do if it were in his power. The sergeant, however, saw it, and my telegraphing too, as I found out afterwards, though he pretended he did not. I was inspected by him, and reported perfectly sober; on which he was ordered to conduct me to my room a prisoner.

I might have been in my room half an hour—not very cheerful either, considering the occurrences of the last two hours—when I bethought myself of my sword-blade, and that it would be advisable to bring it away from the guard-tent in case of accidents; so I sallied out with that intention, but I had not got a dozen yards from my room when I came plump on to the sergeant-major and sergeant again.

"Oh!" cried the sergeant-major, "breaking your arrest!" and he called lustily for two men to take me to the guard-tent, and thither I was accordingly conducted.

The sergeant-major, who was not a bad sort of fellow in general, this evening had, unfortunately for me, been imbibing slightly; and he had this peculiarity in his cups—it could not be detected in his manner or conversation, but he was always intensely "duty-struck" at those times. He started off at once to the captain's quarters, roused him up, and gave such a glowing description of my being out with a drawn sword, and afterwards breaking my arrest, that I firmly believe he thought I was a most dangerous character to be allowed to remain loose, and that the most proper place for me was a cell. He succeeded in imbuing the captain with the same idea. I was, therefore, placed in an out-building which answered the purpose of a prison, and in which one of the mutineers of the 1st Cavalry was already confined.

Behold me, then, installed in the same cell with a rebel who was waiting for death! A small lamp burning dimly in a niche in the wall; he chained up in a corner; I stamping up and down the floor; and a sentry posted outside with a loaded carbine. There seemed, in spite of the serious aspect affairs were beginning to wear, something so absurd and ludicrous in taking such care of me, that I could not resist roaring out with laughter.

My fellow-prisoner, who hitherto had occupied himself with intently staring at me from underneath the *gutterie* in which he was huddled, wondering probably what crime I had been guilty of to be considered a fit companion for him in his retirement, now inquired the cause of my appearance there. In reply, I gave an account of my adventure with the sword-blade; the other parts I, of course, suppressed. This naturally led him to imagine my proclivities were somewhat truculent, and, on his questioning me more closely, I am afraid I told him a vast number of fibs which I will not insert here lest my character for veracity be questioned.

I thought I had now an excellent opportunity of cultivating his acquaintance, and ascertaining how rebel affairs stood; I therefore boldly declared I was a rebel, and a Mahomedan to boot! This rather surprised my quondam friend, for he had not, I imagine, met many *Feringee* Mahomedans. He proceeded at once to put my religious principles to the test, and the satisfactory manner in which I answered his questions apparently convinced him that I was not only a *bonâ fide* Mussulman but a green-turbaned *Hajee*.

We were soon on the best of terms, and discoursed very learnedly on various subjects connected with Mahomedanism, and the relative merits of the Soonis and Sheeas. I was, of course, of whatever opinion he was in this case; perfectly coinciding with all his views on the subject. By-the-way, I forget now which he was, Sooni or Sheea; but that is immaterial after this lapse of time.

The whole of this I looked upon as a capital joke, for I naturally

115

concluded I should be released in the morning; but I was fated to be most grievously disappointed. Morning came, and with it, instead of my release, the order that I was to be kept in the cell till the head-quarters of the regiment arrived, which was expected in the course of three or four days with other reinforcements. This was something beyond a joke. The captain, it seems, thought my adventure so too, and did not consider himself competent to release me under existing circumstances.

I had now plenty of leisure to reflect over recent events, which did not tend to make me very cheerful. What had become of *Harini*? What would be done to me on the arrival of headquarters? For, however absurd the whole affair might appear, in a military point of view it was very serious. There was nothing for it, however, but patience. Those four days seemed interminably long, but I shortened them as much as possible, and relieved the melancholy monotony of my thoughts by talking and listening to my fellow-prisoner.

At length the reinforcements arrived, and immediately there was a rush of those who had friends in the troop to the bungalow, to hear the news, and, as a natural consequence, some of them—not having yet come into contact with the rebels—came to look at the one with me. On seeing me also in the cell inquiries would be made as to what I was doing there, to which I invariably replied that I was put there to "pump the prisoner," and the men, knowing I was an adept in the language, went away perfectly satisfied with my account, till they were undeceived by those who knew the real particulars of my imprison-ment.

The morning after the arrival of headquarters I was marched a prisoner to the "office-tent," and charged, firstly, with "breaking out of cantonments after watch-setting, and having in my possession a drawn sword," &c.; secondly, with "breaking my arrest." In reply to these charges I briefly related the truth, omitting, of course, the romantic part of the affair. After being severely reprimanded by the colonel for not setting a better example to the men, I was released; very glad to get off so lightly.

A few days after, a parade of the whole of the troops took place, to witness the execution of a rebel by blowing him from a gun. This was my fellow-prisoner. Previous to being blown away he had to march past the different ranks, which he did with a firm step and erect car-riage. As he passed by my troop I met his eye, which seemed to say: "Well, I'm very glad to see *you* are all right, at least." His position and mine, at this moment, reminded me greatly of the "butcher and baker."

He marched boldly, to the gun, planted himself firmly at the muzzle, remarking that he did not want to be tied. The word was given, and in a moment my four days' companion was scattered in every direction.

For the information of readers who may not know how a man is blown from a gun, I will briefly relate it. The prisoner is generally tied to a gun with the upper part of the small of his back resting against the muzzle.

When the gun is fired, his head is seen to go straight up into the air some forty or fifty feet; the arms fly off right and left, high up in the air, and fall at, perhaps, a hundred yards distance; the legs drop to the ground beneath the muzzle of the gun; and the body is literally blown away altogether, not a vestige being seen. As there were several blown away from guns at Aurungabad, some of my old comrades will remember this particular one, not only from the fact of my having been in prison with him, but from the remarkable words made use of by him, and which were read on that parade: "If I *live*, I shall be an *avenger*; if I *die*, I shall die a martyr."

I never heard nor saw any more of *Harini*; what became of her I suppose I shall never know. More stirring scenes afterwards caused me to forget, partially, the circumstances of my adventure with her; but, even now, there are times when I recall with a sigh her bright eyes and winning ways, and I wonder what was her probable fate. Poor little *Harini*!

CHAPTER 23

Lahore—Bhopal Contingent

Our force remained in Aurungabad till it was properly organised for effective work in the field; we then left,[1] proceeding in the direction of Central India; and our march through the different districts, no doubt, had the effect of tranquillising the respectable and well-disposed, and of being a sort of check on the lawless portion of the various populations.

It is needless to describe the wild and romantic scenery of jungle, plain, and mountain we passed through, over a tract of country not often crossed by the British soldier. Among the many places deserving note may be mentioned Ajunta, with its *ghaut* and magnificent scenery; the caves of Ellora; the battlefield of Assaye; Aseerghur, one of the strongest fortresses in India; and numerous other places. Suffice it to say that we crossed the Nerbudda at Hoosingabad, marched on to Bhopal, the capital of the petty state of that name, and proceeded to Sehore, a large town distant from the latter place twenty-two miles, where some regiments of the Bhopal Contingent were stationed. Here we halted for a time.

Circumstances afterwards told us why we halted at that place, but for the present we remained in profound ignorance, and fancied we were wasting precious time in inglorious ease when we could be better employed against the rebels farther up the country, of whose atrocities rumour brought so many fearful accounts; but our superiors knew what they were about better than we did, as will be seen in the sequel.

One morning at stable-hour we were ordered to have our arms in the lines, and the horses ready saddled and bridled; the men were, however, to be strip-shirted, as was usual at that hour, and busy about

---

1. The 1st Brigade started for the relief of Mhow on the 12th July.

the horses, but to be prepared to mount at a moment's notice. Of course, we thought something out of the common was afoot, and speculated among ourselves what the upshot was to be. While thus engaged, the different regiments of the Bhopal Contingent marched by the head of the lines, and we began to suspect that our preparation had something to do with them, though in what manner we could not conjecture.

They had no sooner passed the lines than we were quietly ordered to put on our jackets and arms, and mount. In a few minutes we had formed up in front of the lines; we were rapidly "told off," and at once, with the infantry and artillery belonging to the force, marched off in the direction the Bhopal Contingent had taken.

We soon reached a large plain, where we saw the Bhopal troops going through a field day. It seems the whole—or some portion, rather—of the Contingent had previously mutinied, and had assisted in the outbreak at Indore; hut, on hearing of the expected arrival of our column, had returned to their duty, thinking their delinquency would not be discovered, or, if discovered, would not be punished. They were, however, destined to be mistaken; but the difficulty was, to disarm them without bloodshed or loss to us. Finesse was resorted to to effect that object, and the result showed that it succeeded to a nicety.

Brigadier Mayne ordered a general parade of the Contingent, as if for inspection, and putting them through a field-day. The troops unsuspiciously marched to the parade-ground, were inspected by the brigadier, and put by him through a few manoeuvres. We now appeared on the scene; and the erewhile mutineers—concluding, probably, we were to join in the manoeuvres, but had arrived late—showed no suspicion. The brigadier then formed them up in line, and gave the infantry the order to "pile arms"; this they did; he then gave the word "right-about face," and marched them some distance to the rear.

This, being a common movement, did not excite their suspicion; but no sooner were they a sufficient distance off, than a portion of our force was rapidly placed between them and their weapons; at the same time our guns, loaded with canister, were turned on their cavalry and artillery; thus the whole lot were rendered powerless.

In the meanwhile we had surrounded the parade-ground to prevent anyone from escaping; our followers collected the arms, and placed them in *hackeries* that were at hand; the cavalry were ordered to dismount, which they did most unwillingly, and their horses were led away by our grooms. The whole of the Contingent were then ordered to peel off their uniforms, and were marched prisoners to a camp prepared for them, and strictly guarded.

As it turned out, it was fortunate this plan of disarming them was adopted; for many of the muskets were afterwards found to be loaded with ball, and, under other circumstances, probably many lives would have been lost—and we were not so many in numbers that we could afford to lose even one through mismanagement or recklessness. Thus what threatened to be a dangerous undertaking was accomplished, through tact, without the loss of a man.[2]

Guarding these men caused us a great deal of extra work, for we were nearly always on duty; but the arrival of Sir Hugh Rose, who assumed charge of our force, soon put a stop to this sort of thing. He at once ordered a drum-head court-martial to sit for the trial of the prisoners, and the result of its first sitting was that a hundred and forty-nine of them were convicted and sentenced to death. Not a bad beginning.

The carrying out of the sentence was a little out of the common, so I will relate it as well as my memory will allow me, and, making allowance for some inaccuracy in minor details, I think it will be found substantially correct.

At about 6 o'clock in the evening the hundred and forty-nine men, pinioned, were marched to the rear of the camp. They were drawn up in line; facing them, and but a few feet distant, were the same number of English infantry—most of them recruits belonging to the 3rd Bombays.[3] These were placed, each man opposite a prisoner, and at the word "fire" would each be expected to "polish off" his man. Behind these, on foot, were fifty of us (the 14th) ready to give a quietus with our swords to those of the prisoners who, by accident or any other cause, should not have received it from the infantry.

We could easily see that some of the young fellows forming the firing-party did not half like the job, as it was the first time they had witnessed the shedding of blood, or, rather, were to shed blood themselves—especially in such a manner, face to face—without the excitement which is felt in a battle, and which takes away all its horror. It is, I must confess, unpleasant to shed blood in cold blood for the first time; one can only become used to it in time, and then only do

---

2. I have no means of ascertaining the strength either of our force, or that of the Contingent; but I think they out-numbered us, which made the undertaking somewhat hazardous, and, had they known our intentions, we must have lost many men.
3. 3rd Bombay European Fusiliers.

it because it is one's duty to do so. The infantry felt its unpleasantness, I have no doubt.

Firing-party and prisoners were facing each other; the prisoners thinking, perhaps, of the lives they were so soon to lose, the firing-party of the lives they were so soon to take. The word was given. Now came the awkward part. The rebels knew the words of command just as well as our own men did, and acted accordingly; for at the word "Fire!" some threw themselves down on the ground uninjured, the shot passing harmlessly over them, these prisoners then attempting to bolt—others were, of course, shot down. On the other hand, some of the firing-party—perhaps from nervousness—missed; or, being so close to the men they had to shoot, when they fired, the wads from their muskets set fire to the muslin clothes worn by the prisoners, and there were seen men wildly running about or writhing on the ground in flames.

The sight was very awful, especially as it was by this time nearly dark, and the men looked just like so many demons running about. The moment the infantry had fired they stepped back, and left us to finish the work, which we did in a very short time, not being very squeamish over it either, nor missing a man; for, curiously enough, when the bodies were counted the next morning—and they presented a most ghastly spectacle, lying about in every possible position—they were found all correct, but—there was one over! Instead of the hundred and forty-nine bodies there were now a hundred and fifty![4]

---

4. The "one over" was, I believe, a brother of one of the prisoners, come to see the last of him, and in the *mêlée* must have shared his brother's fate, whether by accident, or purposely, no one knew.

Chapter 24

The Resurrectionist

Shortly after the last post sounded, and when those who were off duty had just turned in, as they thought, for the night, on the night of the executions described in the last chapter, we were startled by an alarming uproar in the direction of the prisoners' camp; muskets firing, shouting, yelling, in fact a regular hubbub appeared to be going on in that vicinity. Of course we were up in a moment, turned out in no time, and anyhow,—some even going "Dagobert fashion,"—and quickly proceeded thither to ascertain the cause.

From what could be gathered, it appeared that the prisoners were struck with dismay on hearing of the deaths of their hundred and forty-nine comrades, and had very gloomy apprehensions as to what would be their own probable fate; thinking, no doubt, that the whole lot would be polished off by similar instalments. They, therefore, hastily made up a plot amongst themselves to attempt escape by seizing a propitious moment and making a general rush for it. Arming themselves with tent-pegs, *lotas*,[1] or anything that came to hand, soon after watch-setting, they dashed out on all sides, thinking to pass the two cordons of sentries that were posted round their camp; but the sentries were on the alert, and shot them down or bayoneted them in all directions, and, with the assistance of the troops from our camp, succeeded in beating the remainder back, so that I do not think one man escaped.

The drum-head court-martial sat every day; as regularly convicted and sentenced detachments of the prisoners to death, and they were as duly disposed of in various manners. One day, I remember, there were thirty to be executed in one batch, of which ten were to be blown away from guns, ten shot by musketry, and ten hung. They were

---

1. Small brass vessels for water, &c.

marched to the place appointed for their execution. On the road there, and previous to the sentence being carried out, one of them, a ferocious-looking Mussulman, spat up to heaven, cursing the Almighty in a most awful manner for allowing the *Kafirs*[2] to thus take the lives of good Mussulmans; this he continued till the very last moment.

The arrangements were soon completed, and, at a signal, ten men were blown away from the guns and sent flying into the air, ten dropped under the fire of musketry, and ten swung on the branches of a convenient tree, kicking against time till death put an end to their struggles. To those who have not witnessed such scenes the account only must appear revolting in the extreme; it is nevertheless true, and to us *then* it was simply so many mutineers the less to have to look after, and we were glad to see them thus summarily and rapidly disposed of. The bodies—portions only of some of them—were collected, thrust into a hole, and hastily covered over, and we returned to the camp.

I may remark *en passant* that of the many executions I have witnessed I have never seen one man who feared or shrank from death; in fact, most of them seemed rather to glory in it—the *mode* of death, apparently, beings the all-absorbing question, not death itself. Thus, to die by being blown away from a gun, or shot by musketry, would be deemed honourable, and would be met without the slightest sign of fear. This callousness of death is the more remarkable, as the same man who would meet it so readily and cheerfully would not do so if he was sentenced to be hung; and he would probably bellow like a bull, and evince the greatest cowardice, if one but gave him a box on the ear. How this paradox is to be explained I have not the least idea—except in the case of hanging, which is a disgrace—and leave it to others to account for this singular combination of bravery and cowardice.

Now one of our men, an Irishman named O'Neill (not the Pat O'Niel of a former chapter), having an eye to business, had noticed that some of the executed men had jewellery on their persons. He had noticed, too, that this was buried with them; and he conceived the design of enriching himself by unearthing the bodies and appropriating the jewellery for his own private benefit. He, therefore, procured a shovel, and about 11 o'clock that night he sallied out to the place where the bodies were buried.

He soon discovered the grave, and at once set to work at removing the earth. He himself describes the night as "a beautiful dark night with just a slight taste of a moon hid behind the clouds." He toiled

2. Unbelievers, infidels.

away at his horrible work, sweating at every pore; not so much from the labour, though that must have been arduous, as from the "sort of dhread that was over me," as he expressed it. In spite of his "dhread" he soon got down to the bodies, and was about to pull one out of the confused heap, when he heard some heavy breathing behind him. He dropped the body in great trepidation, and, turning round in the direction of the sound, he saw a monster with a large horned head standing on the brink of the grave and looking down on him at his work. For the moment he firmly believed it was the devil who had come to witness his nefarious proceedings, and was terribly alarmed, or, as he says, "I felt as *wake* as wather."

A little consideration and closer observation, however, as he grew bolder, convinced him that it was only a *hackrie* bullock. Recovering from his fright he again went on with his ghastly work, till, stamping by accident on the stomach of one of the corpses, it gave such an awful groan[3] that O'Neill clambered out of the grave and took his way back to his tent faster than he left it, giving over all thoughts of obtaining the jewellery he had so much coveted, and been at such trouble to obtain. As he said afterwards, "I didn't so much mind the cow wid its horns, though that at first sthruck me all of a hape, but, bedad! whin I hard the black divils benathe me commince to groan, I hopped out of the hole and was off like a 'red-shank!'" It is needless to say that he was often afterwards roasted for his resurrectionist adventure.

---

3. The man's own account; such a circumstance is, I believe, easily accounted for.

CHAPTER 25

Ratghur—Saugor

"A *rupee* I knock that fellow out of the embrasure!"

Bang! Off went the gun, pointed and fired by the individual who made the foregoing remark—or, rather, offered to make the above bet—and away went the shot plump into the embrasure, to the great admiration of the bystanders, and "that fellow" disappeared; whether "knocked out" by the shot, or anticipating such a proceeding if he did not "clear out" of his own accord, and precipitately doing so for fear of that result, we had no means of ascertaining.

Sergeant-Major Murphy was in command of the guns belonging to a "bullock battery"[1] of the Bhopal Contingent attached to our force; and he took as much pride in those guns as if they belonged to a crack battery of the R. A. He was proud of the guns; of his men—even though they were "only nagurs"; of the very bullocks; but, above all, of his skill as a marksman.

It was a treat to hear him stimulate his men on to increased work with such endearing expressions as, "Hoop! Quick! Go it, ye divils! Home wid it, blast yez! or how the blazes do ye expect I can ever hit anything!" His men worked away on such occasions with a rapidity and precision that were truly astonishing, and looked, stripped to the buff as they were (it ought to be rather "stripped to the *black*"), very much like the "divils" they were styled by their affectionate commandant.

Murphy would run from one gun to another as they were loaded, pointing them carefully himself, and, before firing, would kindly inform us what damage he was going to do. "Do ye see that pinnacle

---

1. Batteries in which guns, ammunition-waggons, &c. are drawn only by bullocks; these, from their size, strength, and docility, are often, in some cases, found to be more serviceable than horses, and are much cheaper, and give less trouble.

there? Well! I'm just going to knock it over"; and over went the object aimed at.

"Now, look! I 'm going to dhrop a shot among them spalpeens at that corner, and scatter 'em." Scarcely would the words be out of his mouth when the "spalpeens" *were* scattered. In fact, so good a marksman was he, that the rebels in the fort soon found it out, and were very chary of exposing themselves on the battlements within range of his three guns.

To account for the position we were now in, and the gunnery practice of the worthy Murphy, it is necessary I should "try back a bit." We had marched on to Ratghur a few days before, skirmishing as we drew near the fort, and losing one man after we had drawn up under its walls, by a shot from a matchlock fired from one of the houses near. This poor fellow was the first man we lost, and his death left a widow in the regiment to mourn his loss, and get married again as soon as she possibly could. There was a good deal of desultory popping going on, soon after we had pitched camp, and during the first portion of the night; shots coming from the rebels concealed in the jungle near it. This was, however, eventually put a stop to, and those who were not on duty turned in and slept, confident of the vigilance of those who were on duty.

The next day the fort was partially invested by some of our troops, while the remainder stayed in camp. I went out on picket near the fort, and really I quite enjoyed it. The weather was delightful; we were located under some trees—always ready, man and horse, for whatever might turn up. Our work was not very heavy; it consisted principally in watching Murphy and his artillery practice; lying down in the shade and smoking our pipes, creating our meals; varied now and then by going on sentry. In short, it was quite a picnic party for us, as the nature of the ground round the fort would not allow us to be of much service, beyond doing outlying pickets, &c. As for the infantry, they were at some other places, so I had no opportunity of observing them or their proceedings.

On the 28th January the camp was attacked by the rebels; these were held in check by the pickets till help came, when the rebels were driven back with the loss of a good many men. The fort was captured, most of the enemy having previously evacuated it. As I did not go into its interior, I can form no idea of what it was like; but, judging by its exterior, I should say that it would take a strong force to capture it if properly manned and defended.

One of the Delhi princes—Fasil Khan, if I remember rightly—was captured in the jungle shortly afterwards under rather peculiar circumstances, which I will endeavour to relate. He had escaped from the fort on one side while the other side was being attacked, and was hiding in the jungle waiting for a favourable opportunity to get clear away. This, considering his gorgeous apparel—which he had no means of changing—and the danger of falling into the hands of the Rohillas,[2] rendered the prospect of escape somewhat remote.

While skulking about in the jungle, one of the *coolies* belonging to the hospital saw him, got into conversation with him, pretended a kindly interest in him, and, on the understanding that he should be handsomely rewarded,, engaged to bring the prince a suit of common clothes in place of the handsome ones worn by him; and, in addition, he undertook to supply the prince with a donkey, so that he might pass off as a villager. All these arrangements having been satisfactorily settled, the *coolie* returned to camp, leaving the prince anxiously awaiting his return with the suit of clothes and the donkey.

On reaching the camp, the *coolie*, thinking it might be more to his advantage to report the circumstance, did so. He was directed to keep his promise with the prince, but at the same time a few of our men were also directed to accompany him a short distance in his rear. The coolie found the prince, who quickly put on the clothes provided for him in place of his own, mounted the donkey, and was led by his treacherous guide to the place where the dragoons were in waiting for him. He was made prisoner; and, wearing the dirty clothes of a menial, and riding a donkey, the prince was safely conducted to the camp, where Sir Hugh Rose, after lecturing him a bit, ordered him to be hung over the gateway of the fort of which he had so recently been governor. He was at once marched off, and the sentence carried into effect.

On the 31st the greater part of our force proceeded to Barodia,

2. It was generally believed that a large body of Rohillas were employed in connection with our force, whose duty it was to form a cordon round the camp, and netting all stragglers who approached it (if rebels). These Rohillas were allowed five *rupees* for every head they brought into camp. Their spoils, in the shape of heads, were brought in every morning, and duly paid for. This was one way of catching all straggling rebels, and, no doubt, saved much harassing work for the pickets and *videttes*; but it is probable also that sometimes the head of a harmless villager was brought in for the sake of the five *rupees*, as I cannot see how the authorities could detect the difference between the head of a villager and that of a rebel. This system was said to be carried on, but whether it really was so I am not in a position to say.

where we had an action with a large body of the rebels; these we routed, and returned back to camp the same evening, somewhat tired with our day's work, but elated with our success.

On our march to Barodia a circumstance occurred, which, though apparently trifling in itself, gave us a high opinion of the personal courage of our leader, Sir Hugh Rose, and, perhaps, had more to do with his after successes than he or others may have imagined. I know it made me feel that I would follow him to the devil, if need be, and I know, also, it was the universal feeling of everyone under his command.

He was riding with the advance-guard at the head of the column, which was at the time in the midst of a thick jungle, and he had gone so far to the front that he was passing the skirmishers thrown out to clear the front as well as the nature of the ground would allow, when the sergeant commanding them, seeing the probable danger he was in, said, respectfully, "Beg pardon, General, but you had better let us go first, in case any of the rebels should fire at you from the jungle."

Sir Hugh at once replied, "Thank you, sergeant; but I never want anyone to go in front of *me*." This anecdote being repeated, convinced us of his daring, as his dealing with the mutineers at Sehore, and the prince at Ratghur, did of his sternness and retributive severity.

A few days after we marched into Saugor, and as we passed under the walls of the fort we were greeted by the ladies, who thronged the battlements, with the waving of hands and handkerchiefs (I will not be positive that they did not even cheer us), and our bosoms swelled with pride to think that our timely arrival had saved *these*, at least, from the clutches of the rebels. This was something to be proud of; for the poor creatures had been shut up in the fort for some months, surrounded on all sides by mutineers, and during the whole of that time must have been a prey to the greatest anxiety as to what would be their certain fate if no help came. Ratghur being only twenty-two miles distant, they had heard our guns pounding away, and, no doubt, fervently prayed for our success. As soon as we had settled with the rebels in that neighbourhood—and we were obliged to clear them off as we went—they were gladdened by the sight of our force marching to their rescue.

We had afterwards to avenge the deaths of those murdered at Jhansi and other places, and there was a stern pleasure in doing so, too; but *this* was a greater pleasure, for we had arrived in time to *save* instead of to avenge, and had successfully effected the "Relief of Saugor."

CHAPTER 26

Maltone

Previous to quitting Saugor for Jhansi, whither we were ultimately bound, it was necessary that the country round about it should be thoroughly cleared of rebels, and detachments were sent out to several places in which were bodies of these worthies, for that purpose.

A strong force under Sir Hugh Rose also marched on to a fort named Gurracotta; this fort was in a very commanding position, and was manned by two complete regiments of Bengal mutineers (the 51st and 62nd), a large number of mutineers from other regiments, and cut-throats of every description and caste, so that we might expect some tough work.

Our long and tedious march was made longer by the many delays on the road, as well as from having to proceed very slowly, skirmishing a great part of the way, and halting occasionally to hang or shoot a few of the rebels. We reached the fort towards evening, tired as dogs, and opened on the place next morning. The mutineers replied with vigour, not only with their guns, but they actually made a rush for our guns. They went back, however, minus some of their number, quicker than they came. In this case, as at Ratghur, after blazing away at the fort for a couple of days, the enemy thought it best to flit, which process they speedily put into execution; but did not get off scot free, for they were pursued, and a good many of them cut up by the Hyderabad Cavalry.

Gurracotta was a very strong fort, and might safely have defied our force for a long time, had the rebels only had the pluck to remain and properly defend it. It was found to be well-stored with provisions, there being immense quantities of grain, flour, &c., and a miscellaneous collection of all sorts of loot, evidently derived from English sources, *i.e.* plundered from English houses.

To prevent the rebels congregating there again, part of the walls were blown down; the work of partially dismantling the fort being completed, we returned to Saugor, where we rested while the materiel requisite for our campaigning further north was being got together. During our stay, too, we made ourselves useful by hanging a few notorious characters up to dry, on one occasion five in a row.

Early on the morning of the 27th we started for Jhansi. We had no sooner quitted the camp than notice was given by rockets being sent up from the city; so that the rebels were informed of the exact time of our departure, and could take their measures accordingly.

The next morning, when we started, the same process was repeated, and beacon fires were lighted at intervals on both sides of our line of march till daylight, which showed that we were pretty carefully watched, and the enemy could make no mistake as to our whereabouts. This must have been annoying to the general, but there was no help for it. Several of the parties who lighted the beacons were captured by our men, but they put on an air of simplicity and made excuses which seemed to satisfy the authorities—at any rate they did not hang them—though if the men had been left to their own resources the wretches would have had but short shift.

On the 3rd of March the main body of our force, under Sir Hugh Rose, had a severe encounter with the enemy at Mudanpore Pass, in which they lost a great many men, and out of which we did not come entirely scatheless, several being killed and wounded, and the general having his horse shot under him. It was, however, a most dashing affair, the General routing the enemy, forcing the pass, and achieving a brilliant victory over them.

On this occasion a portion of the force in which I was, under Major Scudamore, was detached from the main body, and ordered to proceed to a place called Maltone; to prevent the mutineers from escaping in that direction; but, excepting a few shots fired at us from some hills covered with jungle on our right, it was nothing more to us than a common march; though, no doubt, our movement had the effect intended, keeping the rebels in the bounds prescribed by the general for them.

We encamped at Maltone, left a few mementoes of our having been there hanging on trees, and the next day marched to join the other portion of the troops under Sir Hugh Rose.

Late at night, while at Maltone, two spies were caught in our camp, these were handed over to the rear-guard, of which I was corporal;

and they were entrusted to me with strict injunctions not to let them escape on the road.

There was not much danger of that; I planted the two spies between a file of the guard, with orders to knock them over if they attempted to escape, and I myself rode in rear of them with the same amiable intention.

One of the spies was a powerful, brawny-looking fellow with a villainous aspect, and a cunning leer of the eye; one who would evidently not stick at trifles, and who would be an awkward customer in an encounter. He had the shaven head of a priest, but he did not look it by any means. By the squareness of his shoulders, expanded chest, and upright gait, I should say he had been a *sepoy*, whatever he was now, spy, *sepoy*, *budmash*, or priest. The other prisoner was quite a lad, with nothing remarkable about him, except that he was perpetually glancing round furtively, as if he expected to see someone, and was annoyed at the non-appearance. This conduct I put down as suspicious-looking.

We jogged along at the rear of the column for some time, when I perceived that we had gradually and imperceptibly increased our distance from the main body, till we were, as the sailors have it, "a long way astern." I at once ordered the men to close up by increasing the pace; but, no; the more I tried to hurry them on, the more the infernal priest seemed determined to lag behind.

I could plainly see there was nothing to prevent him from keeping up with the column, for he was young, strong, and fresh; so that, unless he purposely lagged, in hopes of getting so far in the rear that we might perhaps be cut off, I could conceive no other reason for it. After a while, finding words were only thrown away on this individual, I touched him up in a fleshy part with the point of my sword, just to liven him up a bit and spur him on to an increased pace.

It was worth a trifle to hear the yell he gave on receiving this piece of attention, and the look of rage and hatred he favoured me with, as he darted off at an increased rate of speed for a short time. He, however, soon forgot his "pricking up," and reverted to his former dawdling pace. As nothing would induce him to hurry up, and as he appeared bent on getting us as far as possible in the rear; irritated at finding neither words nor grass were of any avail, I tried to force him along faster by keeping my horse close to his heels.

The horse, as if annoyed at being forced into such close proximity with a spy, commenced being restive, and ended in going through a series of buck-leapings, &c.; in one of his plunges he knocked the man down, and fairly stamped the life out of him, for in less than five minutes the fellow was dead; spitting up at me and cursing me with his last breath.

This put a stop to his going on altogether; first making sure, however, that he was really dead, I again started off with the remaining prisoner, who ran like a greyhound, after witnessing the fate of the priest, and we were not long before we caught up the main body again.

"When we got into camp, of course, I reported the circumstance of the death of the spy, relating the particulars, and received the usual reply, "Very good." I handed over the other prisoner to the relieving guard, and never saw any more of him, nor did I hear any more inquiries concerning the villainous-looking priest.

On the 7th we marched into Murrowra, a large town belonging to the Rajah of Shahgur, whose state was here annexed on account of his recent complicity with the rebels in their fighting against us. It was a pleasant sight to see the British flag run up over his fort, and hear, in that out-of-the-way place, the different bands strike up the national anthem. No Englishman, who has not heard that soul-stirring strain in far distant lands, or under similar circumstances, can imagine the effect it has on one's mind, bringing every patriotic feeling into play; home, country, friends, come vividly before one in the first burst of that glorious music, and everyone fervently echoes the words of that melodious prayer, "God save the Queen!"

On we marched (occasionally hanging a few of the rebels by the way), the heat daily increasing, till we came to a place called Chuchunpore, distant from Jhansi about eight miles. Here the force halted, and after resting two or three hours we (the cavalry), the horse artillery, and light field pieces, under Brigadier Steuart, were ordered to advance on Jhansi, which we did through a blazing sun, and bivouacked about two miles from the city, being welcomed with some long shots from the batteries, which, however, at that distance, did no harm. The next day (the 21st March) the main body, under Sir Hugh Rose, arrived. He at once proceeded to reconnoitre the place previous to investing it.

I believe there was not a man of us—as we contemplated this stronghold of villainy where so many of our countrymen and women had been butchered under such awful circumstances—who did not thirst for the time to come when he could take vengeance on their murderers, and who did not inwardly register a vow to do his best to avenge their unhappy fate. I know I did.

CHAPTER 27

Jhansi—No Quarter

I am not sufficiently well up in the topography of the suburbs of Jhansi to be able confidently to state the precise spot in which my troop was posted in the investment of the city; nor have I the remotest idea where the other portions of the troops were placed, beyond such vague directions as the right or left attack. Suffice it, that we found ourselves located somewhere about a mile from the city walls; and that between us and them were some very pleasant, cool-looking gardens, which formed an agreeable shade to, and a convenient lurking place for the rebels to fire at us from, and into which some of us occasionally went to do a bit of skirmishing, and either kill them or drive them out.

My troop, the K, under Captain Brown, numbered about sixty men; we were expected to cover a certain portion of the city, to see that none escaped; or to turn out at any moment and on any emergency. Consequently, we were never out of harness; sleeping in front of our horses, which were always ready saddled and bridled—never having the bits taken out of their mouths, night or day, except a few at a time for feeding purposes, or to give them a drink in comfort; so that it came harder on the horses than it did on us.

As for ourselves, I don't think we were able to change our clothes, or have a wash, for about a fortnight, and it may be imagined that we were rather dirty, and that a bath would have done the whole of us good; but we couldn't even peel off to wash our faces, to say nothing of the elaborate luxury of a bath. As the old soldier remarked in a previous chapter, we were "as black as buck-sweeps" (whoever or whatever they may be). Yet, somehow, in spite of this and the dreadful heat, none of us fell sick, and all of us seemed to enjoy the life we led. I know I did, heartily, and should have enjoyed it infinitely more if I

134

could have bathed daily.

In the daytime, lounging about in the lines near our horses was varied by an occasional hurried turn out, or a skirmish in the gardens; and it was worth the chance of a stray shot, to ride under those shady trees, or catch glimpses of our sunburnt faces and rough appearance in the crystal waters of some miniature lake, which one could fancy was the bathing-place of *houris*. I have often thought how delicious it would be to have a swim there; but in general we were too much occupied in "potting" and "sticking" to think much of *houris* bathing, or the beauties of scenery.

Six privates and myself had gone down there one day in charge of a young Irish officer of my troop, named Beamish, and had caught a party of *sepoys* in a small building. They had retreated up a narrow staircase, which was only wide enough for one to go up at a time, and could easily have kept us at bay if they had not been apparently panic-struck at our appearance. We had all dismounted, and our leader was soon busily engaged pulling the *sepoys* one by one down the stairs by their "hind-legs" (as a comrade observed), and handing them over to our tender mercies. This amusement highly delighted Cornet Beamish, who, when he had finished, declared it was much better fun than "drawing badgers."

This business being over, we mounted, and were retiring from the gardens, when a shot was fired at us from the branches of a large tree under which we were passing, fortunately without hitting anyone. On looking up, we saw upwards of twenty armed rebels in the trees, whom we should have entirely overlooked but for that shot. We at once dismounted, and set to work at potting them. This was capital sport—better even than "drawing badgers"—for they could not get away, even if they wished it ever so; and if one was missed by accident, he was "still to the good," perched on branch, for another shot. One by one, our human game came down to the ground with an awful thud; and if they were only wounded with the shot, the fall from the tree was quite enough to settle them, without any more of our assistance.

I had just fired my carbine and brought down a stalwart *sepoy*, when another of the "birds," unperceived by me, slid down a tree, and rushed at me with his drawn sword. My carbine was discharged; I should not have time to throw it down and draw my sword; so I made the best of it; faced him with my empty carbine, and easily parrying his blow, dealt him one in turn with it, driving the hammer right into

135

his temple, at the same time snapping the stock of my weapon off with the force of the blow. My shooting was thus put a stop to, but I determined I would get another firearm before I left, and eventually I secured a blunderbuss which had been pointed at me—and which, luckily, missed fire—containing about a quart of bullets; this I took home in triumph, as a substitute for my broken carbine.

I had an old *ghora-walla* who particularly delighted in this sort of work; and who, I believe, would have gone through fire and water to serve me—perhaps his own interests as well. At any rate, I found him of great service in many ways. For instance, he had managed to loot a couple of milch cows, and always before the *reveille* sounded at morning, on the line of march, he would bring me a *jambu* of warm milk and a *chupattie*. He used to ride one of these cows and lead the other, and if not another *ghora-walla* was up when we reached camp, after a long march, my old fellow was sure to be there to take the horse the moment I stepped out of the saddle. This in itself was a great consideration, for it is not an agreeable thing to have to wait for one's *ghora-walla*, as anyone who has been on the line of march in India knows.

The old fellow used to like following me when we went into these garden skirmishes; and if I knocked over a rebel—wounding him only—he made no bones of finishing him off by inserting his long knife in the fellow's ribs; at the same time rifling him of anything he had on his person. The proceeds of his looting he used fairly to divide with me; often bringing me, as my share, gold *mohurs*, ornaments, &c. It was a great advantage to me to have so ready a follower; for if—as occurred often—we had to skirmish on foot, he was always there to take charge of the horse.[1]

At nights, in addition to the usual sentries and *videttes*, perhaps a couple of dismounted parties, of six men each, and each party commanded by a corporal, would be placed in ambush, to cut off anyone attempting to escape from the city. This duty would be carried out so effectively that the guards, *videttes*, and ambush parties—generally numbering only twenty or so—would, in one night, show two or three hundred bodies as the result of their night's work. I would defy a cat to pass where we were. All the men used to like this sort of work, as there were some very nice pickings to be made—everyone

---

1. The captain afterwards took a fancy to the old fellow through seeing how carefully he attended me, and took him from me to be his groom, but the obstinate old man would not serve the captain as well as he had served me; and the captain pronounced him a stupid, and dismissed him, forbidding him to come near the lines.

endeavouring to escape from the city always carrying all the money and valuables they possibly could.

I will try to give an idea how these ambushes, &c. were conducted. In the lines sentries were always posted; near to the gardens a line of mounted *videttes* were placed; these either remained stationary, or each one rode alternately to his right or left-hand man, as the case might be during the night; relieved, of course, at two-hour intervals, and visited often. On each flank of these was the dismounted ambush, carefully concealed behind bushes or stones. These would listen intently for every sound that came from the direction of the city. By and by a party from thence would be heard stealthily approaching; these would be allowed to advance without interruption till sufficiently near to make sure of them, when the ambush would give them the contents of the carbines, and rush out on them sword in hand, and those who were not knocked over in the discharge, would either fight or bolt, as the case might be.

This performance might possibly be repeated several times during the night; and sometimes as many as fifty would come at the same time. This, however, made no difference to us, we attacked them all the same, and invariably got the best of it—as *we* had the advantage of them in being prepared, if *they* had the advantage of us in numbers.

Sometimes they fought very fiercely, and with all the energy of despair, and there was quite a miniature battle going on; cutting, slashing, firing, shouting—quite a hubbub. Some of our fellows got very nasty sword-cuts in these night encounters; for it *is* awkward work—in spite of any amount of skill one may possess with the sword—to be able to guard one's self with any degree of certainty, from such indiscriminate slashing and thrusting in the dark. Those we killed during the night were collected in the morning, and burnt to prevent any unpleasantness arising by letting the bodies lie and get putrid.

While besieging Jhansi, and during the whole of our operations there, we had orders to take no prisoners—in other words, to give no quarter, to kill every man coming from the city. At any rate, if this order was not actually issued through the proper channels, it reached us by other means, and was acted on and carried out to the fullest extent. Consequently, independent of our desire to have vengeance on the murderers of our people, we were not hindered by red-tape from following our inclinations that way; and we were not very particular as to when, where, or how we killed all we could lay hands on.

One day some of the men caught a priest wandering about, and, by way of a change, determined to try him by a "private court-martial." This was very soon assembled, and, after doing a little in the "Judge and Jury" line, the priest was sentenced to be hung. He was forthwith dragged to the end of the horse-lines, where there was a very convenient tree, "built expressly for a gallows," as one of the men facetiously remarked.

One of the horses' head-ropes was speedily placed round the victim's neck, and he was hauled up into the tree. It took the poor wretch a long time to die, he not having had the advantage of a "drop"; this was soon rectified by one of the men climbing the tree, sliding down the rope, and dropping on the victim's shoulders, which effectually stretched his neck and put him out of his sufferings. They then left the man hanging there, and retired to the tents, or in front of their horses, where they soon forgot the revolting tragedy they had been engaged in.

One of the men, however, thought he would hoax the man who had finished the scene by sitting on the hanging man's shoulders; so, when he saw the coast clear, he cut the corpse down, and, the body being yet limp, he placed it in a sitting posture at the foot of the tree with its hand to its head, as if scratching it, or as if he was in a "brown study." He then rushed off to the executioner, exclaiming, "I say, Blinkee!" (the man's nickname) I'm blest if the old priest you hung hasn't got down out of the tree, and he's sitting at the foot of it, scratching his head."

"Well, I'm damn'd!" cried Blinkee, "I'll soon make him scratch his head, to some purpose too!" and seizing hold of a tent-peg, he rushed off and gave the corpse a tremendous blow on the head with it before he perceived the hoax that had been played on him.

To most readers this scene will appear brutal and revolting, and it would have appeared so to us under other circumstances; but the reader must bear in mind what had recently occurred to our country-women in this very place, the awful accounts we had heard of what they had had to put up with before their deaths—of the manner in which they were finally butchered—of what we had ourselves actually seen—and the surprise will cease; or, rather, the wonder is that those we caught were not treated worse in the desire of gratifying our vengeance.[2]

---

2. A good many rebels were executed at Jhansi; some who had given themselves up, expecting pardon if they gave all the information they could to Sir Hugh Rose. They were disappointed. A story is told of one who (Continued next page.)

Lest the reader should imagine the above description to be somewhat overdrawn, it is only necessary to say that we were placed in a capital position; that immense numbers, anticipating the fate of the city, nightly tried to escape, and were *stopped*. Some men of my troop could boast of having killed several hundreds, and (I say it with great modesty) I killed many more than one hundred myself during our operations before Jhansi. It must be borne in mind, too, that no quarter was to be given, and I don't think many of the men did give much.

The last few words in the previous chapter were "I know I did"; the last words of this shall be, in allusion to giving no quarter,—I know I didn't.

---

gave himself up, and described the massacre of the British residents, and the atrocities perpetrated on the unfortunate women. Sir Hugh Rose is said to have listened patiently till the man had finished, when he inquired, "And you witnessed all this?" The man replied that he had. Sir Hugh at once called for the provost-marshal, exclaiming, "Take him away, and hang him like a dog! No Indian shall live to say he saw an Englishwoman dishonoured and murdered."

CHAPTER 28

In a Scrape, and Out of One

In the preceding chapter I have necessarily confined myself to what concerned my own troop only, or came under my actual observation. Our sphere of action was, however, very limited, and things were hourly occurring at other places of which we had not the slightest cognizance. For all we knew of what was going on around us, we might almost as well have been at the antipodes. People who have never left their own country, through the medium of newspapers, often are more familiar with the particulars of a siege or battle than those actually engaged in them.

All we knew then, beyond our own little skirmishes, was that there was an incessant pounding going on day and night in all directions—our side shelling and breaching, their side answering us and repairing as well as they could the damage done by our shot.

The shells must have created great havoc in the city,[1] killing numbers of the rebels, to say nothing of the red-hot shot with which they were regularly supplied, and which now and then fulfilled their mission by setting fire to buildings of various kinds, the smoke and flames of which ascending above the walls of the city testified to the effect our firing produced.

The inhabitants must have had a warm time of it, and it is not to be wondered at that they attempted to get out of it; only, as far as concerned us, they invariably illustrated the old proverb of *jumping out of the frying-pan into the fire*—this they did literally, for their bodies were burnt every morning.

---

1. The city contained about 12,000 troops (rebels), and the number of inhabitants would probably not be over-estimated at 100,000. Considering that this was a "native state," where the majority know something about arms, and that great numbers would probably use them, some idea may be formed of what we had to contend against, our force being about 5,000 of all arms.

About this time we shifted our position, and the disposition of the troops was materially altered; for information reached the general of a large army of rebels, under Tantia Topi, coming to attack us, and, of course, rout us, and raise the siege. This advancing army was the same force that had caught General Wyndham, of Redan notoriety, napping, and given him such a lesson in Indian warfare. But they were not going to catch us that way; nor did Sir Hugh Rose intend they should, raise the siege either; but, I suppose, the anticipated arrival of this force necessitated some alteration in the disposition of our troops round the beleaguered city, in order to prepare for and ensure them a warm reception.

At night I was corporal of the outlying picket, immediately connected with the portion of the force in which I was, and it was my duty, alternately with the sergeant, who belonged to another troop, to visit or relieve the *videttes* during the night, and to take them off at dawn.

It fell to my lot to have to do the latter; but the sergeant who made the last round of visiting the *videttes*, just before daybreak, and who ought to have roused me, neglected to do so, as we had mutually done to each other during the night, forgetting all about it, and, lying down in front of his horse, soon dropped off to sleep—for it did not, in our cases, take long to perform that pleasant operation.

Not being roused, I slept the "sleep of the tired," till the sun was quite up in the heavens; when I woke up of my own accord, rubbed my eyes, stared round, and, in a moment, not only was wide awake, but was also awake to the fact that, by over-sleeping myself, I had kept the *videttes* on an hour after dawn, and had unwittingly committed a very grave military crime.[2]

I immediately jumped on my horse, and trotted off to bring them in, explaining to each of them in turn the reason I had kept them on so late. All were satisfied with my explanation except one man, who, when I came up to him, pulled out his watch to time me, remarking that I had kept him on duty an hour too long, and that he should report me for doing so. Irritated at this, when I knew it was no fault of mine, but of his own sergeant—for the man belonged to the sergeant's troop—I told him not to *talk* of reporting me, but to *do* it when we got back to the lines, and that I would myself take him before the

---

2. *Videttes* should always be brought in at the first break of day for various reasons; but chiefly, that the enemy should not know precisely where they are posted during the night, which they would if the men remained on after daylight.

adjutant to enable him to do so.[3]

After picking up all the men, we rode into the lines, where, seeing the adjutant, I remarked to the man that he could now report me if he wished; as he *did* wish to do so, I conducted him before the adjutant, and told him the man wished to make a report against me. The adjutant inquired of the man what it was, and on being told it was for keeping him an hour longer on his post than he ought to have been, the adjutant had no other alternative than to place me under arrest; he, therefore, without more ado, ordered me to my tent, a prisoner.

I dismounted, and travelled off into my tent, very much annoyed at the circumstance, but soon did my best to forget all about it in sleep, and succeeded admirably. Towards evening, however, things began to assume a different aspect; a good deal of buzzing seemed to be going on in the lines, and there was the unmistakable sign of preparing for something. The men and horses were all in readiness, I could perceive, for a sudden turn out; for the army of rebels was advancing on to Jhansi, and might come at any moment, and when they *did* come there was sure to be some fighting going on; while I at the same time should be cooped up in a tent, a prisoner, and out of all the fun of it.

I spoke to the sergeant-major about it, requesting him to see the captain, and, get him to exert his influence with the colonel to settle my case summarily, so that I might be released; but I was told that the colonel couldn't be bothered at a time like this, and that I should have to remain a prisoner till the expected fighting was over.

Not if I knew it, however. I would have been "all there," even if I had to break my arrest again, of that I fully made up my mind. I wouldn't have it thrown up to me, hereafter, that I was absent from a "go-in" through being a prisoner. I, therefore, ordered the old *ghora-walla* to have my horse ready and my weapons in the lines at his head; and I myself remained dressed, ready for anything that might turn up.

The troops were just then "falling in," and I was standing at the door of the tent, staring at them, and ruefully cogitating what I should do, when I saw the colonel walking backwards and forwards at the head of the lines. A bright idea struck me. Why shouldn't I make a direct appeal to the colonel? I couldn't be much worse off than I was at present. I no sooner thought of this plan than I proceeded to

---

3. It is a rule in the service not to *threaten*; if a man considers himself hardly dealt by, he can always report the circumstance without talking about it; or if a man commits an offence, a non-commissioned officer should not *threaten* to send him to the guard-room, but *do* it.

carry it out. Regardless, therefore, of military etiquette, or of breaking my arrest—for it was neither more nor less—and, reckless of consequences, I immediately went up to the colonel, saluted him, and stood before him as if wishing to address him.

Colonel Scudamore, who was considered a very stern man and a strict disciplinarian, stared at me, and then abruptly inquired:

"Well, what do you want?"

This did not look very favourable; but I began, "Beg pardon. Colonel, I'm a prisoner—"

"What the devil are you doing here, then?" interrupted he. After a pause, he said sharply, "What have you done?"

I then briefly related the circumstance of my arrest, and begged him to release me, so that I might be present at the anticipated engagement, as I should not like to be absent from it by being left in camp at a time like this.

"That's all very well," again interrupted he; "but if I release you now, I may not be able to catch you again, and you'll escape your punishment."

I told him, when the affair was over, if I lived, I would willingly consider myself still a prisoner, and receive any punishment he might award me; that I did not wish him to release me now to escape merited punishment, but that I should not like to be absent when an engagement was taking place, as I should not only be laughed at by my comrades, but it would tell against my future promotion, as perhaps some commanding officer, on looking over the *Defaulters' Book*, might fancy I shirked out of my duty on such an occasion as the present.

I could see by an almost imperceptible smile twitching about the colonel's mouth, when I told him I would come back to receive my punishment, that he was not angry; indeed, I fancied that he seemed to approve of what I had done by coming to him in the manner I had, though he could not, of course, express his approval. It was evident he did not think any the worse of me, for, turning away, he said sharply, "That'll do, you're released."

I saluted, and hurried back to the lines as happy as possible in my suddenly acquired liberty, hastily put on my belts and arms, mounted my horse, and took my place in the ranks, to the infinite surprise of the sergeant-major, who thought I ought to have been snug in my tent, and who rode up to me demanding what I was doing there on parade.

"I'm released, sergeant-major," replied I.

"By whose order?" inquired he, doubtingly.

"By Colonel Scudamore's."

"Oh! I must ascertain about that," exclaimed he. I suppose he did made inquires about it, and found it all correct; for I never heard any more of the matter, and the case was, I believe, never entered in the *Defaulters' Book.*

This little adventure, so far from doing me any injury, was rather of service to me; for it gave the colonel a good opinion of me, that I wasn't one who would willingly be absent when the services of every available fighting man were so much needed.

Chapter 29

The Battle of Betwa

I was not sufficiently in the confidence of Sir Hugh Rose to be able to get a sight of the plan of the Battle of the Betwa; so in a strategic point of view it would be simply absurd in me to attempt to describe it, except in the crudest and roughest manner, as can only be expected from one in my position.

We had stood to our arms the whole of the night, with the enemy very close to us, so close that we could see their fires burning and hear the usual camp noises; in some places, it is said that the rebels taunted our men, threatening what they would do on the morrow, so it is evident they were confident of success.

As well as I could make out, the general's arrangements were as follows:—Brigadier Stuart was sent to our left with a small force to attack the enemy in flank, or prevent them from making a flank movement and entering the city; while Sir Hugh Rose with our main body was to oppose that of the rebels, which outnumbered us as much as twenty to one,[1] and were stronger than us in guns.

The different troops engaged in the investment of the city remained as they were, and were to keep the rebels in the city from sallying out to attack us in rear, or joining their comrades who were coming to their relief, and *vice versa*. To carry out this amiable purpose, guns loaded with canister were placed so as to sweep all the approaches from and to the city.

At daybreak our guns opened fire on the enemy, which they returned with interest, and there was such blazing away that it seemed to shake the very ground beneath us. We could, when there was a bit of a lull in the firing, just to let the smoke rise, hear the booming of guns,

---

1. Our force opposed to the enemy numbered about 1,200; the enemy numbered about 25,000.

too, in the direction of the city, and could fancy our comrades were all employed there. Occasionally there was heard the yells of triumph coming from the devils in the city, in anticipation of our certain overthrow—so they thought—and I must confess we (the men) fancied things looked very black against us; but we had every confidence in our leader, and were not going to be easily beaten, in spite of numbers or appearances.

Could anyone have taken a bird's-eye view of us on that morning,[2] it must have been a glorious sight.

Actually three battles going on at one time. We, under Sir Hugh Rose, with our small force fighting twenty-times our number, charging again and again, through the blazing jungle too (for the enemy had set fire to it, thinking by that means to cover their retreat and to check us, so that it was literally and truly warm work); Brigadier Stuart, on our left, fighting and routing his lot; and Colonel Gall with his guns hammering away at the city, which seemed like a veritable hell peopled with yelling incarnate fiends who vomited forth fire and flames.

I know we all thought, at one time, when Sir Hugh put himself at the head of a squadron of ours and led the chaise himself, that even he fancied things looked doubtful; and that if he was to be overpowered by numbers he would at least die a glorious deaths at the head of his troops in a charge! I know, too, that those he led thought he was only leading them to certain death; but they felt proud at going to death in such company.[3] It was a glorious sight to see them thundering along headed by the general and Captain Prettejohn, the latter of whom was bareheaded, and who fought and shouted like a demon; one minute, and they were among the enemy, and all that was to be seen was a confused mass of flashing swords and bayonets, struggling men and horses, and hoarse shouts of rage. From this seething struggling mass our men emerged victorious, for the result of the charge showed that an act of daring and personal bravery on the part of a leader (an act

2. The man in charge of the telegraph on the top of a high hill in the neighbourhood of the battle, and between the battlefield and the city, must have had a. capital view; at the commencement of the battle we were on the side of the hill nearest the city, with orders to keep our position there; but the telegraph-man, by shouting and frantic signs, indicated that a portion of the rebels were coming over a gap of the hill, when, though against orders, the captain led us over the hill just in time to stop them from breaking through and getting behind our pickets round the city; this was thought a capital movement.

3. Captain Prettejohn.

not often done—a commander-in-chief to lead a charge) will some-times change defeat into victory, as it did in this case.

The rebels were thoroughly routed in this charge, and turned and fled; were rallied, formed up again, to be again charged and routed; and yet again, only to undergo the same infliction, losing all their guns,[4] and finally bolting in the greatest confusion, pursued by our men, who cut up great numbers of them, stopping only at the River Betwa from sheer exhaustion.

Numbers of the enemy who escaped our swords were drowned in attempting to cross the river; the whole of the ground passed over by our men was strewed with the bodies of the enemy; and at the lowest estimate it was calculated that 1,500 of them must have been slain, and no doubt the wounded were at least as many more.

Our cavalry and artillery bore the brunt of this severe engagement, my regiment suffering the most, from the nature of the conflict being a succession of charges and hand-to-hand fights. The troops returned to camp pretty tired with their day's work, but highly delighted at having achieved so brilliant a victory over their vaunting foes.

It may not be inappropriate to insert the telegram Sir Hugh Rose forwarded to Government after the battle in this place; it may, in its very brevity, give a better idea of things than my rambling descrip-tion (indeed the chapter would not be complete without it). It runs thus:—

This morning, at daybreak, the force under my orders fought a general action with the so-called Peishwa's army, and, by the blessing of God, gained a complete victory. The rebels are stated to have numbered from 20,000 to 25,000 men; they were un-der Tantia Topee, Nana Sahib's relative, and their object was to relieve Jhansi. I did not discontinue the siege nor investment of Jhansi, consequently the force with which I fought was ex-tremely weak. The rebels, amongst whom were the Grenadier regiment and another regiment of the Gwalior Contingent, fought, except the cavalry, desperately; but I turned their left flank with artillery and cavalry, and, after making two stands, they broke and fled, defending themselves individually to the last.

I pursued them to the River Betwa, taking all their guns, eight-een in number, and an English 18-pounder of the Gwalior

---

4. Some of the guns had the name "Wyndham" painted on them.

Contingent, drawn by two elephants, an 8-inch mortar, and quantities of ammunition, including shells, 18-pounder shot, ordnance park, and two more elephants. Two standards were also taken. The enemy tried to stop our pursuit by setting the jungle on fire, but nothing could check the ardour of the artillery and cavalry, who galloped in pursuit across the country in flames. I cannot calculate at present the enemy's loss in killed; but it must have been very great, as the country is strewed with dead bodies, chiefly. those of *sepoys*. As I now shall be free from the attacks of a numerous attacking army, I hope to conclude speedily the siege of Jhansi.

CHAPTER 30

The Fall of Jhansi

I could not give an accurate account of the storming and capture of Jhansi, even if I wished to do so, as I had not the honour of being one of the stormers; it is, therefore, beyond my power, and it would be absurd were I to attempt anything like an elaborate description of it. Contenting myself, therefore, with merely a brief allusion to it, I must confine my remarks to delineating, as well as I can, what came under my own observation.

Suffice it to say that the infantry stormed and took the city on the morning of the 3rd of April, after some very hard fighting, and the loss of a great many men—the 86th in particular suffering severely, every officer, excepting one, being either killed or wounded, and upwards of 200 men rendered *hors-de-combat*—so that there must have been sharp work going on. Although the city was taken on the day of the storming, street-fighting was kept up for three or four days, after which the city might safely be considered ours.[1]

Luckily for our force, the enemy evacuated the fort after the city was taken, as it would have cost much time and the loss of many men to reduce it. As regards its strength, Sir Hugh Rose in a telegram observes:

Jhansi is not a fort, but its strength makes it a fortress; it could not have been breached, and could only have been taken by mining and blowing up one bastion after another.

Another writer observes:

The position was strong, the town having a good wall[2] mounted

1. The number of natives killed in the city is estimated, variously, at from 3,000 to 6,000. I don't suppose the latter number was far out, when one considers the indiscriminate slaughter which took place, and that no quarter was given.
2. The wall was of granite, and about twenty-five feet in height.

by many guns; above the town, and constituting a separate and very formidable point of defence, frowned the huge castellated palace of the former *rajahs*.

The reader is recommended to read the glowing description of the storming and capture of Jhansi in the pages of *The History of the Indian Mutiny*.[3]

On the night of the attack, the *Ranee* made her escape from the city on horseback, with about 2,000 followers, and fled in the direction of Jaloun, though how she managed to pass the pickets was a mystery. She was pursued for a long distance, but succeeded in getting away, with the loss of about two hundred of her escort, who were cut up by our men.

The *Ranee* is described as being a very handsome woman about 24 years of age, of a licentious disposition, selecting her lovers indiscriminately from all ranks, and, when tired of them, sending them off about their business, or promoting them according as they ingratiated themselves in her favour; in short, she was a second Catherine of Russia. Were it not for the atrocities, however, that she committed, or caused to be committed, she would have had the sympathies of everyone; for she was a perfect Amazon in bravery, heading her troops, mounted like a man, just the sort of dare-devil woman that soldiers admire.

When we first arrived in Jhansi, she made overtures to Sir Hugh Rose, wishing to have an interview with him. Sir Hugh, however, knowing all her antecedents, gave her to understand, through her messenger, that if she came near him, woman and princess as she was, he would certainly hang her. She had nothing for it, therefore, but either giving herself up to be hung, or fighting to the death. Finding herself driven into a corner, she preferred doing the latter, and fought against us again and again till she was finally killed at Gwalior. Could the history of this remarkable woman be written, it would no doubt present some very strange features.

While the fighting was going on in the city, we were not idle outside, but polished off numbers as they tried to escape, and it is probable more were killed in that way than in the assault of the city and the subsequent street-fighting. There was this difference, however: those *we* had to deal with were fugitives *flying* for their lives, while the troops in the city had to do with desperate men *fighting* for their lives, and determined to sell them dearly. So that there was less danger in our

---

3. Vol. 2, pages 289-296.

work—not but what we had a sharp encounter now and then, where it was staring one another in the face, and *feeling* our way with our swords[4]—but most of it was simply killing.

One day twenty-four of us, under Cornet Beamish, went, from one end of the city to the other, without the walls, skirmishing, and we must have killed an immense number one way and another. We rode into one courtyard in which there were at least 200 armed men; these fellows were so panic-stricken at our appearance, that they threw down their arms, and allowed us to butcher them with our swords till we were actually tired with the slaughter. I don't think we left many of them alive!

Once or twice in our progress through the gardens, we had some little encounters on foot; for the wretches, after firing, would dash under the bushes, &c, and there was no getting at them unless we dismounted. In one of these bouts I had just put my sword into the ribs of one of these fellows (an artilleryman), and he clung to the bare blade, holding it in his body,[5] and cutting his fingers to the bone in doing so, at the same time making frantic attempts to bite my leg; fortunately my boot protected it, but he held my trousers in his teeth as tenaciously as a bull-dog would, and I had to use the spur of my other boot in his face to make him relinquish his hold. This will give some idea of the savage nature of our warfare in these little skirmishes.

It was blazing hot on that day, and, what with the violent exercise and the sun, I was parched with thirst; and I could imagine that I did not have a very prepossessing appearance when I came to a well, where were two women drawing water—one an old one, the other young and good-looking. I rode up to the well and desired them to draw me a drop of water; the younger woman stared vacantly at me as if she were frightened, or did not properly understand me, and I repeated the demand for water in a louder tone. I suppose the poor thing, judging from my appearance, must have fancied I was a very savage fellow

---

4. There was comparatively little danger in having a brush with rebels single-handed, for they only made cuts; these are easily guarded—indeed, one has but to guard the first, and then insinuate the point of one's sword into the opponent. Experience has shown the advantage of pointing over cutting: a person might receive a dozen cuts and recover from them, but nine out of ten *must* die from a point through the body. I cannot prove this by statistics, but for all that it *must* be a fact.

5. The popular belief among natives is, that *drawing the weapon out* causes death (not plunging it in, I suppose), and that as the weapon comes out, so also does the life-blood; but all the while the weapon remains in, the recipient of it will live. This man evidently wished to have some satisfaction at the very last moment of his life.

and wanted her life; for, without a word, she plunged into the well, to the horror of the old woman, who commenced wringing her hands and bewailing her loss.

I was truly sorry for the poor creature throwing her life away like that, and would have helped her out again with great pleasure, had I thought she would have accepted my help, but knowing by experience that she wouldn't, I contented myself with desiring the old woman to draw the water, which she did at once, and in great trepidation.

At this time Cornet Beamish came up, and told one of the men to loosen his horses' heel-ropes, and try to get the young woman up. He might have spared the trouble; for she preferred drowning in the well to being saved by the *Feringees*.

Everyone felt sorry for the fate of the poor creature; but I felt that I was, inadvertently, the cause of her death—though had anyone else come up first, she would probably have done the same thing. I felt more sorry for her death than I did for all the men that I had killed[6] on that day.

In our skirmishing many of the men made some very good loot. I was rather fortunate that way myself. I noticed a fellow, on one occasion, nursing a bundle with very great care, which led me to think it contained something more valuable than clothing, so I gently inserted my sword into his ribs, dismounted, and took care of it for him. I had no time to inspect the contents then, but hastily tumbled out a lot of gold-*mohurs* into the holsters of my saddle; and dropping a *snake*,[7] through the network of which I could see the "yellow dross" glitter, into my haversack, I mounted and went on with my skirmishing. Now and then, when I had occasion to trot, I had the mortification of seeing some of my gold *mohurs* dancing about in the wallets, and some of them rolling out.

---

6. Numbers of poor women, whose husbands, brothers, or fathers had been killed by us, voluntarily followed us and our fortunes. What were they to do? Having left the city, they could not return; their friends being killed, they had no protectors or home, and in time they came to look on the very men who had killed their relatives—and whom they had been taught to look upon with abhorrence and hatred—as their protectors and friends. I have often conversed with some of these women, and it was amusing to listen to the account they gave of the tales their former friends had instilled into them concerning our ferocity—to females in particular. I need not say they were agreeably undeceived, and probably enjoyed life more now (low as they had fallen, morally) than ever they did before, and would not have had their caste restored, and return to their former way of living, even if they could have done so.

7. A long net-work purse, worn round the waist as a sash.

After the day's work was over, and we had returned to camp, I inspected my prize, which consisted of about a quart of gold *mohurs* (I did not bother about counting them); and quite a valuable collection of gold bangles, gold ear, nose, and finger rings, studded with jewels, were contained in the snake. Yet they were, after all, comparatively worthless to me, and I was glad to get rid of them as soon as possible; for the weather was so hot that I could not be burdened with the weight of them. I could not give them over to anyone's care, as they were *loot*, and would be handed over to the prize-agent; if I left them in my kit, they might at any moment be stolen, or the baggage might be cut off, and my prize with it; so I gradually got rid of them by buying luxuries, in the shape of delicacies, wine, beer, &c., at exorbitant prices, and finished the last of the rings long after the campaign was over.

I think it will take many years to efface from the memory of the inhabitants of Jhansi the awful retribution which fell on that place to avenge the murders perpetrated there. I have avoided interlarding these chapters with sensational descriptions of the frightful atrocities inflicted on European women here and at other places. That relating to Jhansi has been officially contradicted—the official version being that the victims were simply butchered, without being blackened or dishonoured. Let us hope the version may be true; but from my knowledge of Indian character, and conversations with natives, I believe that they *did* have to suffer horrors, as bad, if not worse, than any description yet given of them. I only hope I may be mistaken. The authorities, no doubt, had good motives in hushing the matter up as well as they could, out of kindness to relatives, &c.; yet, in spite of this, the stern appalling truth *will* peep out here and there from amidst the glossed-over accounts written by officialdom, and make one's very blood boil at the thought of what the poor victims must have suffered.

But enough of this. Everything was done for the comfort of the wounded, Sir Hugh Rose himself visiting them constantly; but the intense heat proved highly detrimental to them, greatly retarding their recovery, in some cases causing wounds to mortify, which, had the weather been cooler, would probably never have happened.

There was a good deal of sickness, too, among the men; it almost seemed as if the constant excitement of the past fortnight had alone kept many from succumbing, and the moment the fighting was over sickness ensued. Be that as it may, one thing is certain, from the time the fighting ceased sickness began to be rife in camp.

A remarkable case occurred here which may not be undeserving of mention. An old soldier of ours, named Harry Gordon, reported himself sick one morning, but could describe his symptoms no more lucidly than that "he felt as if he wanted to be always lying down." The doctor (a recent importation) bade him go back to his duty, saying it was simply laziness, and that there was nothing whatever the matter with him. The man went away indignant at the doctor's insinuation, exclaiming,

"There's a pretty d——d doctor, to tell me I'm lazy, and that there's nothing the matter with me! A lot he knows about his business. I'm d——d if I don't go back and die, just to show what a b——d fool he is!"

He kept his word, for in less than an hour he was carried to the hospital, dead! The doctor had thought the poor fellow was scheming, when in reality he was dying.

Shortly after, the place containing the bodies of the murdered Europeans, numbering sixty-seven, was enclosed by a wall, and the funeral service read over them. This solemn duty being performed. Sir Hugh set to work to prepare for further campaigning, our ultimate destination being Kalpee, and towards the end of the month we found ourselves marching in that direction.

CHAPTER 31

Koonch.—"Not Dead Yet"

We began now to suffer much from the heat of the weather; and, as if to add to our discomfort, we continued, through some sapient red-tapery, still to wear our winter clothing. Fancy an Indian hot season, with the thermometer at 115° to 120° in the shade, constantly being exposed to the sun at—I will not venture to say how many degrees—and wearing the identical sort of woollen clothing we should have worn at home in the bitterest winter!

I should say this sort of thing cost us a good many men, who, had we been supplied with clothing suitable to the season, would probably have been living now. What with heat, little rest, and other concomitant evils, we began to feel somewhat knocked up. We used generally to march during the night, so as to come to our halting-place by daylight or shortly after, in order to avoid as much as possible the intense heat of the sun; and I must say Sir Hugh Rose did his best to avoid exposing us unnecessarily—a consideration which we fully appreciated, and were not slow to expose ourselves when required, as we always felt sure it was unavoidable.

We were marching on to a place called Koonch, where, it was understood, a large body of rebels were posted, and whom it was anticipated we were to encounter on the morrow. We proceeded on during a great part of the night, occasionally halting for a short time to rest our horses; and so much were we fatigued by the recent forced marches, and the heat of the weather, that no sooner were we off our horses' backs than we were down on the ground and fast asleep in a moment; we did not want any tucking in, nor such superfluities as pillows. No one who has not experienced the same can imagine the delightful feeling of dropping off to sleep in that manner, nor the intense annoyance felt at the first blast of the trumpet, which calls the troopers from their temporary forgetfulness, to shake themselves, mount their horses, and wearily jog on their way again.

After one of these short halts, we were marching along in silence; each one, perhaps, buried in his own meditations, thinking of home, friends, and other sentimental nonsense, undisturbed even by the click of the *chuck-muck*, for there could be no enjoyment of the pipe at such a time. I was dreamily cogitating in my own mind the probable events of the coming morrow, when I noticed a *dhoolie*, borne as usual by four bearers, noiselessly proceeding by the side of my horse.

There being nothing unusual in this, I at first scarcely paid any attention to it, but perceiving that its close proximity made my horse fidgety—a thing unusual with him—and that persistently it neither went ahead nor dropped back, but kept so near to my horse, and in such a silent manner, for I now for the first time noticed the silence of the bearers, I could not avoid being struck with its singularity. This was rather a remarkable thing, they are generally the reverse of silent, and usually have a peculiar sort of cry or chaunt, as I distinctly remembered, having taken the trouble to translate some of their chaunts, to my own entire satisfaction, on first arriving in the country, and before I knew anything of the language; my rendering was thus—free, of course:

1st Verse.

Front Bearers	*He's so heavy!*
Rear	*Damn him!*
Front	*Ain't he heavy!*
Rear	*Damn him! damn him!*
All	*Ai! Ai! Oh! Oh!*
"	*Damn him! damn him!*

2nd Verse.

Front Bearers	*Shall we drop him?*
Rear	*Damn him!*
Front	*We'd like to drop him!*
Rear	*Damn him! damn him!*
All	*Ai! ai! Ho! Ho!*
"	*Damn him! damn him!*

I am inclined to think, from the fact of the rear bearers having principally to sustain the chorus, and doing it, too, so energetically, that they also sustain the heaviest portion of their burden. This is suggestive, and is a fit subject for scientific research; the compiler of statistical tables relating to it would, without doubt, confer a boon on society in general, and be amply rewarded for his own trouble in compiling them.

To return to my own particular *dhoolie*. I spoke to the bearers, and told them either to go on or back; but receiving no answer, I rode my horse a yard or two out of the ranks, to make them, and they retreated as he advanced, the *dhoolie* still keeping the same distance from the horse as before. I thought this somewhat strange; but what was my surprise, on looking closer to ascertain who was the occupant, to see *myself, apparently lifeless, stretched in it!*

Now, I do not consider that I am particularly superstitious—in fact, I believe that I am rather the reverse; but there seemed to me something very remarkable in the circumstance, to say the least of it. Was I awake, or dreaming? I rubbed my eyes to ascertain. I was evidently wide awake; intensely so. Here were my comrades behind and before—or, rather, in front and in rear of me—and there was that infernal *dhoolie* still continuing its noiseless progress by my side, and containing my *other* body, to all appearance defunct.

I could not reasonably tell all this to my comrades, for they would naturally laugh at me. I could not, either, ask anyone if they saw the *dhoolie* (in my own mind I felt sure they could not), for they would just as naturally conclude I was a fit subject for a strait-jacket. There continued the *dhoolie*, however, with my lifeless corpse in it, and my proper, living self riding by the side of it!

This led me to call to mind all the tales of apparitions, fetches, &c., I had ever heard or read of; and I concluded, much to my dissatisfaction, that it was a sort of warning of what was to occur to me on the morrow. So after mature consideration I came to the conclusion that "what *is* to be *must* be;" and, to coin a word, Mussulmanically and philosophically resigned myself to whatever might turn up, even if that operation included my toes. Shortly after, another halt was sounded, and I saw no more of my *dhoolie* nor its ghastly occupant.

Morning brought us near the vicinity of Koonch, with a large body of rebels drawn up in front of it. Our troops were halted, both to rest them and to make the necessary preparations for an attack. Each man was served out with a dram of grog and some biscuit soon after we halted, which met with the treatment it deserved. I had utterly forgotten my nocturnal apparition, and was in capital spirits. I considered myself particularly fortunate, too, in obtaining a good drink of water from Major MacMahon, whose *bheestie* had just brought up a *mussuck* full of it, clear and cold; the Major also let my horse have a drop, which I looked upon as a great favour, as there was not much water procurable just then, which greatly enhanced the value of his kind gift.

For some unaccountable reason—or, at least, for some reason that I was unacquainted with—we were kept waiting for a long time before operations commenced with that portion of the force in which I was, and in that time twelve men of the 71st Highlanders were sunstruck. Poor fellows! just coming out from home, they could not stand the heat so well as those more seasoned to the climate, and they suffered in proportion. During that halt they tried to shelter themselves from the fierce rays of the sun, as well as they could, by spreading towels or pocket-handkerchiefs on the points of their bayonets and huddling under that little bit of shade. We had an advantage over them, for we could sit in the shade under our horses' bellies!

Towards noon we became engaged with the rebels. I am not going to describe the battle—for that is out of my power—but simply relate what happened to myself. As I mentioned before, in the first part of the morning I felt in capital order; but as the day advanced I became sensible of extreme giddiness in the head, a choking sensation in the throat, and a great craving for water, which I eagerly drank, and as eagerly poured over my head and down my bosom[1] whenever I could get the chance. This produced a temporary feeling of coolness that was positively delicious; for the hot wind, blowing through the saturated clothes on the body, became quite cold and chilly.

This lasted, however, but for a few moments, and, of course, I could not always have water poured over me; others wanted it as bad as myself, among the rest Sir Hugh Rose himself, who, but for repeated *douches*, would probably never have survived that day. He was prostrated three times with the unbearable heat of the sun, and as often rose with renewed vigour after receiving the contents of a *mussuck* over his head and body.

To return to myself. I felt very queer, as if I did not care whether I laid down and died, got hit from some stray bullet, or, indeed, what became of me—in fact, I thought it would be rather a good thing to be knocked over, and be out of that terrible sun altogether, and I know that was also the feeling of a good many.

I was on the left flank of the front rank of my troop; next to me rode a lance-corporal, junior to myself, and, in spite of this feeling which I have endeavoured to describe, I had previously asked him to

1. This was a very common practice.

give a look if anything should happen to me. We had already had some little skirmishes with the rebels, and were now ordered to charge a large body of them drawn up on the opposite side of a ploughed field some distance off. This, as near as I can tell, was about 1 o'clock.

Off we started! I have a hazy recollection of madly galloping and plunging over this ploughed field, which was full of trenches—of a good deal of firing, shouting, cutting and slashing, and then all was a blank.

I must have been unhorsed, either by my horse falling with me or my falling off on my own account. In either case I was senseless, and do not remember anything till about 2 o'clock in the day, and the reader will please bear in mind that I say that time advisedly.

On first recovering my senses, I found myself on the ground. I sat up as well as I could, and saw several dead bodies scattered about near me, and not a living soul within sight. The hot glaring sun was striking fiercely on me; no shade anywhere that I could crawl to to escape its awful rays. It was maddening! My God! I would have given the world for a bit of shade, if it were only the size of a cabbage leaf!

On turning round, at some distance off I saw a *dhoolie*, but no bearers. There, at least, was some shelter from this burning sun. Oh, yes! I could get into that, and for the remainder I cared not, so that I was out of the direct glare of the sun. I managed to crawl to it; but, on opening it, I found a dead body lying in it. I suppose I must have revolted from the idea of climbing in on to the top of him for shade. Who he was, or what he was, I never knew from that day to this, but I left him in possession of the interior of the *dhoolie*.

Leaving him thus, I cast my eyes about for some other means of shelter; this, such as it was, I perceived immediately. I remember, distinctly, that the *dhoolie* threw a shadow at the side of it about six inches in breadth, which made me imagine it was about 2 o'clock at the time. I remember, too, that I eagerly thrust as much of my head as I possibly could into that little six inches of shade, and I remember no more.

In the charge over that ploughed ground my troop lost several men. It was full of pit-falls, and these were not discovered till we were right in the midst of them, when, of course, the only thing to do was to plunge through in the best way we could. One man had his neck fairly broken by his horse coming down with him. Strangely enough, too, this man, and another, also, who was killed, had been for some time undergoing imprisonment, and had only been released that morning to take part in the action, as a great favour, and at their own earnest entreaty.[2]

I cannot here resist telling an episode which occurred after this. Some of our men were in hot pursuit of the rebels; they had galloped for many miles, cutting down whatever stragglers they overtook. What with the heat of the sun and their violent exertions, they must have been maddened with thirst, when, to their great joy, they came up to a well. Most of the men carried a *lota*[3] attached to the pommel of the saddle, supplied with a long string to enable them to lower it into wells and draw water. On perceiving the well, they quickly dismounted, unslung their *lotas*, and lowered them into it; when, to their surprise, some of them were cut from their strings, and the men were greeted with a volley from the bottom of the well.

Some dozen or so of the rebels—there being only about a foot of water in the well—had concealed themselves there; and, had they let the men quietly draw the water, they might have remained undiscovered. As it was, the men were bound to have water at any price; so they kept firing over the edge of the well into it till the rebels were nearly all killed, when they were astonished at hearing a voice in English cry out, "For God's sake, pull me up!" One of the men immediately lowered his horse's heel-ropes and pulled up the individual, who turned out to be a half-caste, probably a band-master of some native regiment. His English, however, did not save his life, but rather hastened his death. In a moment half-a-dozen swords were through him. He fell, crying, "Oh, my God, has it come to this!" It *had* evidently come to that; no mercy could be shown to one in his position; his being able to speak the English language and having English blood in his veins rendering him doubly culpable, and a thousand times worse than the villains with whom he was leagued.

Our men now turned their attention to the well, and having ascertained its occupants were all dead, or at least quiet, peaceably drew up their water for a refreshing drink, but, much to their disgust, it was quite red on account of the shallowness of the water and the number of rebels who had been killed in it. Necessity has no law. They were parched with thirst; they *must* drink, blood or not blood, and they *did*.

On this day I was not the only man who was sun-struck, numbers of others shared the same fate, and several of them died—I think seven or eight. I was picked up afterwards and carried to the hospital tents

2. The names of the men were Steadman and Townsend.
3. Small brass drinking-vessel, carried by all natives.

senseless, and remained so for two days—at least, I remember nothing for that time; and I must have been *particularly* senseless, for I was returned in the despatches as *dead*. These despatches were copied in the papers, and sometime after I had the satisfaction of reading an account of the engagement and my own death. I procured one of these papers, and forwarded it home to my friends, who, I believe, have it in their possession now, as a curio.

This was not all; it was customary in the regiment to put a stone up over any comrade who died, and on the news of my death some of my old comrades in the depôt at Kirkee raised a subscription and put a tombstone up in the cemetery there to my memory. It was with a mournful pleasure, some three years after, I visited the hallowed spot, and, standing opposite my own headstone, read the following:—

Sacred to the Memory
of
Corporal LE Warner,
H.M.'s 14th (King's) Light Dragoons,[4]
Who Lost His Life
At Koonch,
On the 7th May 1857.
This Stone was placed here
By
Some of his Comrades.

Now I think there is something very remarkable in this; for I have paid for my own coffin, I have been returned as dead, I have moralised on the shortness of life over my own tombstone, and "I'm not dead yet!"

---

4. Since then the 14th has become a Hussar Regiment.
5. Miss Lydia Mary Fay.

CHAPTER 32

Kalpee and Galowlee—Ravings and Misty Recollections

Those days during which I was senseless may be considered as sponged out of my existence—wiped out altogether—leaving a perfect blank. When I did come to my senses it was not to a full possession of them, but a languid dreamy consciousness of where I was and what was going on about me, not by any means distinct. I saw everything as if the objects were enshrouded in mist, or as if a veil of some gauzy texture were drawn between me and them; I forgot what I saw immediately or remembered it only partially as one remembers a dream or phantasm of the brain. The sound of voices appeared smothered and indistinct, as if my ears were stuffed with cotton. It was fatiguing to look at anything, it was more fatiguing still to listen to their mutterings. There was one sound I did like to hear, however, the sound of water; but, oh! how delightful it was to lie there and feel the cool water dashing on my burning head and trickling over my face and bosom.

No melody was ever so sweet as the music of that drip, drip, drop, drop, was to my delighted ears; all other sounds were swallowed up and lost in that limpid harmony; all other feelings were dead save the exquisite feeling of relief its coolness produced on my heated brain. It must be Elysium could one only die to the sound of that delicious trickling music.

I have an indistinct recollection of being carried on the road—I don't know what it was in—of the dreadful sun being on every side of me, trying to get at me and scorch my brain up; but, thank God! I could defy it. I had carefully put my head in the shade, and the shadow must grow broader and broader as the sun descended and grew weaker and weaker. That was a good idea of mine, wasn't it, putting my head in the six inches of shade? Why, it must be a foot now! and by and by, as *he* sinks, my whole body will be in the shade, and then I can laugh at the sun—he will be powerless to hurt me. Oh! yes, I'm well protected now and can almost defy the sun. I don't know whether I used to talk at all; but sometimes I had very pleasant dreams, generally of home, &c.; I am, however, inclined to think they were merely waking dreams.

I have a confused remembrance of being in a tent which was full of "sun-strokes,"[1] some of whom seemed to unaccountably disappear and be replaced by others,—of dreamily listening to the delirious ramblings of men, as they tossed on their beds and flung their arms about, fancying they were talking to friends at home. As soon as one began to talk of home *his* place was sure to be vacant very shortly. I remember that very well, but was not at all surprised at it. Who wanted to hear about *his* home or friends? Why don't he lie quiet and *dream* of them if he likes, and not interrupt others in *their* dreams? I can remember the horror I felt when I first thoroughly understood that I was in hospital, the dread of dying there, my restless desire of being out of it and among my comrades. What the devil did they bring me here for? There's nothing the matter with me, I won't stop in a d—d hospital! Everybody dies that comes here. I so worried the doctor who attended me with repeated asseverations that I was quite well and wanted to go out, that he discharged me; but the senior doctor would not allow it, as he said it was simply sending me out to die. So I had to remain; but I pestered *him* too, till at length, I believe, he was glad to get rid of me, and discharged me from hospital.

Although I was once more at my duty I was still very hazy in my ideas, and every time I lay down to sleep I became delirious; on several occasions the men roused me from my raving sleep and wanted me to go back to hospital, but such was my dread of that place that I swore I would never go there unless carried. I soon discovered that if I did not lie down when I slept I was free from delirium, so I hit on the plan of sitting cross-legged like a tailor, and sleeping in that position. This plan I followed for many weeks; and at length I got so used to it, that for a long time I could sleep in no other position.[2]

---

1. One man was actually struck through the tent. He was in the hospital with some other complaint when this occurred, and could not have been exposed to the sun at all.

2. The habit of sitting cross-legged became so natural to me, that (continued next page.)

For weeks, too, although performing all my duties regularly, I did everything mechanically, as if I were in a dream, and can only imperfectly remember passing events, even though I was present and acted my part in them.

Most curious, too, I never remember eating anything at this time, though, of course, I must have, done so; but certain particular drinks of water or tea I had *then* are as vividly impressed on my mind *now* as if I had them but a few minutes ago, and I can recall the peculiar flavour of the beverage, and the influence it had on me, even to this moment.

I have a faint recollection of the sufferings of that awful march on to Kalpee: of men and horses[3] dropping down from heat and exhaustion; of men, unable to go any further, crawling under any bush by the roadside that afforded the slightest shelter, and being picked up dead or dying and carried on; of our fellows sometimes giving some of the infantry a lift on their horses to help them a bit of the way on the road, while they themselves walked; of men of the 71st dropping by the dozen and being carried into our tents senseless, dead, and dying.[4]

---

even now I cannot entirely break myself of it, and often catch myself sitting cross-legged on my chair at table.

3. Many of the horses were sun-struck, or dropped. dead with heat and exhaustion; it was pitiable to see them sometimes dragging themselves, they must have suffered terribly, both from heat and want of water. A man would always divide his water with his horse, and let him drink out of the bottle first, too. I have seen a man cry at the death of his horse, who, perhaps, would not have shed a tear at the death of his nearest relative; nor is it astonishing that a soldier should love his horse, when one considers how much, to a dragoon, depends on him. I have been greatly impressed at noticing great rough fellows treating their horses as tenderly as if they were babies. Nor would I give much for the dragoon who did not love his horse and treat him kindly.

4. The case of this regiment was particularly hard, as they had but few camp followers, and, I think, no cooks—the men themselves having to cook their meals in the blazing sun, after a long march. Our men were able to show them many little acts of kindness, which they never forgot. We were well supplied with camels and elephants, and our tents and baggage generally kept up to us, and reached the camping-ground almost as soon as we did; we were, besides, mounted. They had to march on foot, and having bullocks only to carry their tents and baggage, which were always late in arriving; and but for the shelter we afforded them in our tents, the poor fellows would, after a long march, have had to wait for hours in the burning sun for their baggage to come up. On one march in particular, dozens of the men were carried into our tents, senseless—struck down by the sun, heat, or fatigue—and the doctor of the 71st actually cried at the sad spectacle, exclaiming, "My God! my God! what will become of my poor men! I shall never forget your (the 14th) kindness to them."(Continued next page.)

I can remember there being no water on the road; and men falling out maddened with thirst, and scraping in the dry bed of a river to get a drop of the precious liquid;—eagerly drinking the filthy tepid puddle which tasted more sweet to the parched lips than the purest nectar;—the thronging of men and cattle round a well which was rapidly growing shallower till it finally became dry, struggling, fighting, and crying for water;—men dying of thirst with swollen tongues lolling out of their mouths and bolting staring eyes;—and one man being sun-struck, and, *knowing* it, in his delirium fiercely stabbing with his sword up to heaven, and daring the Almighty to come down and fight him like a man, and not strike him "foully with this b——d sun."

When we reached Galowlee I can remember something about being short of water there, and having to shift our camp through it; and something of the Jumna being only a few miles off; of the enemy being between us and that glorious river, that we must beat them to get to it, and that we *did* so too.[5] I can remember the enemy harassing us in the daytime when the sun was hottest, and they knew that many of us must succumb to its blasting influence (it seems to me now that we were perpetually out in it, repelling their attacks—now on this side the camp, now on that);—the enemy sometimes coming so near that the shots came into camp and apparently from all sides at once, as if we were surrounded; there were repeated turns out and fights against awful odds in the blazing sun, and finally a glorious victory and the capture of Kalpee.

I can see the river now, glittering in the bright rays of the sun like a broad waving band of molten silver; the ravines leading to it thronged with men, horses, camels, elephants, bullocks, all possessed of one craving desire—water; all rushing to the river to quench their burning thirst with its cool waters, to lave their wearied bodies in its clear bosom. I can remember seeing the whole, men and cattle, rush pell-mell into the water, which they drank to repletion, and afterwards wallowed in—the men, regardless of their clothing, mingling with their four-footed brethren in the stream.

That indulgence cost the lives of many of the poor beasts, whose swollen carcases choked up the ravines they had so recently descended; water which they so much needed, and so much craved for, thus,

---

The men of the 71st never did forget; forever afterwards any man of our regiment would be welcomed, even if a stranger to them, with open arms, and treated with the greatest hospitality.

5. The enemy had sworn to sweep us into the Jumna.

instead of saving life, causing death, through having been drunk too copiously.

In the fort at Kalpee[6] we found an immense quantity of munitions of war and other stores, which proved that the enemy did not anticipate our capturing the place, or they could easily have removed them.

Parties were sent out in pursuit, under Colonel Gall and Captain Abbot, respectively; these killed great numbers of the flying enemy, besides capturing all their guns, camels, elephants, horses, &c., with which they returned in triumph to camp.[7]

Colonel Gall deserves something more than a passing notice, and, though I disliked him personally, I cannot refrain from expressing my admiration of him as a soldier and a daring officer. He was a short, spare, sallow-visaged man; but in his little frame was an immense amount of courage and endurance. He, I believe, gloried in danger, and would face anything or everything—the devil himself. He had so much confidence in himself, and the men, that he used to say, "Give me the 14th, a regiment of infantry, and a troop of artillery, and I'd sweep the whole of India." The general had a high opinion of him, and was constantly sending him on expeditions in which tact, daring, and endurance were required, and he was invariably successful; chiefly owing to the good example he showed to his men.

When he was seen to leave the camp with a small party, it was a common saying, "There goes Gall to look for a fight," and he generally found it; on foot or on horseback, in a charge, or a storm, it was all one to him. The infantry who had been out with him spoke en-

---

6. Why we should have had to march over a thousand miles, and fight our way through all sorts of odds to capture Kalpee, when an overwhelming British force was for months only a few miles distant from the place, I, nor, I believe, anyone, can conceive; but such was the fact. It may have been part of a deep-laid plan; but I must confess it was too deep for my limited comprehension.

7. The general presented one of the elephants to the 14th. This elephant used to march at the head of the regiment. The men subscribed for its maintenance, and that of its keeper, who used to be gorgeously dressed, and sit in state on the elephant's back, on such occasions. He knew every man, woman, and child of the regiment, and would throw up his trunk and salute any of us with a trumpeting sound; but, strange to say, he would never notice the men of the 6th Inniskillings, who tried to make his acquaintance. On one occasion he killed a horse belonging to the 6th, by crushing him to death against the wall of his stable. When we were leaving India it was found impossible to take him with us, and he was sold, to our great regret, as we had all grown to like Kooglia, and he would have caused quite a sensation at home, marching at the head of our regiment.

thusiastically of his reckless daring; he was "too brave," and on one or two occasions, when on foot, the men have actually had to hold him by force, to keep him from rushing to certain death. He had received a sword-cut on the wrist during the Sikh War, in endeavouring to seize a standard, which rendered his right hand useless; he thought to get over that, however, by inventing a sword which could be fitted to his *wrist*; this, after a trial or two, he found did not answer, so he had to give it up, and use his *left* hand. In leading a charge—either against the enemy, or at a field-day—he would turn round in his saddle, and say, "Now, men, you are quite at liberty to gallop over me—if you can!"

He was always so splendidly mounted that that was an impossibility. In riding, his light frame seemed to grow out of the saddle; as the old soldier caustically remarked, "he sticks to the saddle like a sick monkey on a yard-arm!" He was reported never to undress, but always to sleep booted, belted, and dressed, ready for a turn-out on the instant; and this would appear to be true, for at the first blast of the trumpet he would appear riding down the lines fully equipped, as if he had been waiting for the trumpet to sound. I am not his biographer, or I might write a volume concerning him, but I will conclude with observing that, though he was not very popular among his own men as a commanding officer, every man of us admired him for daring as a soldier.

Our force having completed the work it had been destined to do, it was ordered to be broken up, and the troops distributed to different stations, and kept under cover during the remainder of the hot season, to enable the men and cattle to rest and recruit their strength after so much hardship and suffering. Sir Hugh Rose also announced his intention of going to Bombay on sick certificate, he being thoroughly knocked up with his recent exertions, and took leave of the troops in the following General Order, which I insert for the reader's perusal:—

Field-Force Orders by Maj.-Gen. Sir Hugh Rose K.C.B.

Camp, Calpee, 1st June 1858.

The Central India Field Force being about to be dissolved, the Major-General cannot allow the troops to leave the immediate command without expressing to them the gratification he has invariably experienced at their good conduct and discipline, and he requests that the following general order may be read at the head of every corps and detachment of the force.

Soldiers! you have marched more than a thousand miles, and

taken more than a hundred guns. You have forced your way through mountain-passes and intricate jungles, and over rivers. You have captured forts, and beat the enemy, no matter what the odds, whenever you met him. You have restored extensive districts to the Government, and peace and order now reign where before, for twelve months, were tyranny and rebellion. You have done all this, and you have never had a check.

I thank you with all my sincerity for your bravery, your devotion, and your discipline.

When you first marched, I told you, that you, as British soldiers, had more than enough of courage for the work which was before you, but that courage, without discipline, was of no avail; and I exhorted you to let discipline be your watchword. You have attended to my orders. In hardships, in temptations, and in dangers, you have obeyed your General, and you never left your ranks.

You have fought against the strong, and you have protected the rights of the weak and defenceless, of foes as well as of friends. I have seen you, in the ardour of combat, preserve and place children out of harm's way.

This is the discipline of Christian soldiers, and this it is which has brought you triumphant from the shores of Western India to the waters of the Jumna, and establishes, without doubt, that you will find no place before which the glory of your arms can be dimmed."

I will venture to say there was not a man of the force whose bosom did not swell with pride and exultation when he heard this order read. Those few words effectually effaced all remembrance of suffering and hardship, leaving only the pleasure of being thought by our general worthy of his praise.

I commenced this chapter raving, and I verily believe I shall have to finish it raving, but in a very different manner. What a wonderful effect a few appropriate words have; here I am, ready to go through another lot.

CHAPTER 33

Gwalior—Roasting Alive

We were destined to be disappointed in our expectations, there was to be no rest for us yet; the idea of resting during the remainder of the hot months was still in perspective, and so distant we could hardly see any prospect of it at all.

News came that the Ranee of Jhansi and Tantia Topee had managed somehow or other to scrape a large army together, with which they had proceeded to Gwalior, and had fought a battle,[1] in which the Maharaja's troops had been worsted, though led on by himself with great gallantry; that the whole of his troops, with the exception of his body-guard, had gone over to the rebels, who had succeeded in taking the fort, city, and the *Lushkar*, with all the guns there were in the former, and the immense treasure there was at the latter place. His fort, city, palace, throne, and treasure gone, and his troops gone over to the rebels, the *maharaja*, with a few of his faithful body-guard, had fled to Agra, while the rebels busily occupied themselves in trying to organize a government for their newly acquired possessions.

The general no sooner received this startling intelligence than he determined to forego his sick-leave, and once more take the field, at any risk. It would not do to leave such a strong place as Gwalior in the hands of the rebels, as it would nullify all our hard-earned victories by becoming a rendezvous for the disaffected from all parts of India, and probably cause a great deal of time and trouble to capture. There was also the fact that a loyal prince was driven from his throne and country by the rebels, after gallantly fighting against them; so it was evidently the duty of our Government to let the Pandys see that they should not have it all their own way, and that if we were quick to avenge ourselves on our foes, we were as equally quick to render

1. This battle was fought on the 1st of June.

169

assistance to our friends and strike a rapid blow in their behalf.

Off we went again, on the 6th June, and after some very severe marching, under a rather warm sun,[2] on the 16th we reached Morar cantonments, where a large body of the rebels were posted, waiting for us. They had not long to wait; for Sir Hugh Rose, with his usual dash, went in at them, tired as we were, at once. After a few rounds our troops advanced, driving the enemy before them out of the cantonments and killing numbers of them, the 71st in particular going in at them with the "cold steel" in a *nullah* where a lot of them had ensconced themselves, as if they did not intend being driven out; neither were they, for after some fierce hand-to-hand fighting, in which the 71st lost an officer and several men, they left the *nullah*, but not till every rebel in it was killed.

It was frightfully hot, and the sun struck down on us with awful power, buttoned up as we were in thick woollen tunics. The officers were requested to speak to the colonel to allow us to take them off and strap them in front of the saddles; but the permission was not granted, as it was not "regimental or soldierly"; so that there we were in front of the enemy, stifling, sweltering, gasping, and not half so effective as we should be were we allowed to peel off—because it was not "regimental." I don't know how it was, but some man, I suppose, watching his opportunity by seeing some movement amongst the rebels, and anticipating a corresponding one on ours, suddenly pulled off his tunic, and in a twinkling every man of the regiment peeled off. Just at this moment we were ordered to change position, and throw out skirmishers, so it was impossible to order them to be put on again, and for some time we were so fully occupied potting the enemy that it could not be done.

The colonel, like a sensible man, seeing the unanimous feeling of the regiment, took no notice of the men all being strip-shirted, and afterwards issued an order that for the future we might turn out in that manner. This was really a great boon, better late than never; and if it had been done months before, it would probably have lessened the death-roll of the regiment. It had more advantages than one, too; for not only did we feel cooler, and could use our arms better, but, I believe, the enemy thought we had an addition to our force, in a regiment of dragoons wearing white jackets, when it was simply one of the old ones strip-shirted.

2. One day the thermometer was reported to be 130° in the shade; the Lord only knows what it was in the sun I know it was warm.

I cannot here avoid giving a word of praise to two classes of hard-worked followers, without whose assistance we should have been awkwardly placed, and who faithfully served us during the whole of the arduous campaign. These were the *bheestie-wallahs* and the *dhoolie*-bearers. The former, whether on the line of march, or in front of the enemy, were sure to be in attendance, and contributed greatly to our comfort, by moistening our parched lips with a timely drink of water, or pouring the cooling liquid over our burning heads and down our bosoms; the hot winds blowing through our wet clothes, giving such a sense of coolness and exquisite pleasure—even if only temporary—impossible to describe. If water was to be had, there the *bheesties* were with it, no matter what the risk. The *dhoolie*-bearers, too, were always close up to the column, ready to bear off a wounded or sun-struck man, and often running the risk of being shot in doing so. These two classes of men must have had pretty hard times of it, as the hotter the weather, or the more sick and wounded there were, the harder became their work—in fact, their work was never done; and they ran almost as much danger of being killed as we did, as they were often under fire, and never shrank from their work. I think these poor fellows got medals; if they did not, they ought to have got them, for they richly deserved them.

But to return to Morar. Before the day was over we were in possession of the whole of the cantonments, while the enemy still remained masters of the town and fort, and occupied the heights to the east of it in strong numbers.

Sir Hugh Rose, understanding that great preparations had been made, by throwing up batteries, to check our advance on to *Phoolbagh*,[3] a place about half-way distant between Morar and the *Lushkar*,[4] made a long detour the next night, and joined Smith's brigade at Kota-ke-serai, outflanking the enemy, and coming into Phoolbagh behind them, without much loss; and finally, after some severe fighting, town, fort, *Phoolbagh*, and the *Lushkar* were in our hands, together with up-wards of fifty guns of various calibres.

3. "Flower garden." A garden and palace near the foot of the east end of the fort. The palace was afterwards used as a barracks by the 71st.
4. Literally, "encampment"; but in reality a large well-built town, containing the *maharajah's* palace, and many good streets and buildings; the city of Gwalior was on the other side of the fort, immediately at the foot of it. So that Gwalior proper, or the scene of our operations, were the Morar cantonments or lines, occupied by the Gwalior troops; the *Phoolbagh*, the city, the fort, the heights, and the *Lushkar*. There was no fighting in the latter place.

The Ranee of Jhansi was killed in the attack on *Phoolbagh*, either by a fragment of a shell or a bullet, while directing the movements of her troops. She wore the dress of a mounted officer, as was her custom, at the time she was killed. Her followers burnt her corpse, to prevent it falling into the hands of the British, whom she so mortally hated.

The mutineers had no braver leader than she was, nor the British a more inveterate enemy and obstinate opponent. Her death, but for the atrocities she committed, would have been pronounced "glorious," and she would have been honoured as a brave foe, a true heroine, and a real patriot; as it was, her death rid the world of a beautiful but bloodthirsty monster.

When we rode into *Phoolbagh*, the first sight that met our gaze was enough to make the blood run cold with horror, or boil with rage; for there, hanging *by the legs* from the branches of a tree, were the bodies of two Europeans, naked, except the socks, and swollen to an enormous size; they had actually been roasting over a slow fire! for beneath each of them the fire was scarcely cold. These men were recognised (by the socks they wore) as belonging to the 8th Hussars; their horses had, I believe, fallen in a charge on the previous day, and they had been left on the ground, unnoticed, perhaps. As far as I could see, there was no wound on either of them, and they must have been hung up in that manner to make their death as lingering and as maddening as possible—their heads being about a foot above the fire. What the poor fellows must have suffered, God only knows. They were at once cut down and buried.[5]

Brigadier Napier was despatched with a flying column of cavalry[6] and horse artillery, numbering about 600 men; with this handful he performed one of the most dashing feats on record. He came up with about 8,000 of the enemy, under Tantia Toopee and the Nawab of Banda, charged into them, cutting up great numbers, and capturing all their guns (twenty-five) and an immense quantity of ammunition. It must have been glorious to have seen that charge—men, horses, and guns thundering on into the ranks of the enemy, sweeping everything before them! Other flying columns scoured the country in all directions, cutting up the enemy wherever they came across them.

On the 20th, the *maharajah*, who had been desired to return in haste to Gwalior, was escorted by all the troops in camp to his capital.

---

5. I heard that there were five bodies found hanging in a similar manner. I only saw two; the others must have been at some other place.
6. 14th Dragoons and native cavalry.

Scindia was attended by Sir Robert Hamilton and Sir Hugh Rose and his staff, and the brilliant *cortége* riding up the broad street leading to the palace must have appeared very imposing to the inhabitants, and taught them to respect the power that had brought their monarch back to his capital. Sir Hugh having restored Scindia in triumph to his throne and kingdom,[7] and having seen everything satisfactorily arranged for the disposition of the troops, fairly exhausted and worn out, again resigned command of the force, and started for Bombay on the 29th, the guns from Gwalior fort booming out the announcement of his departure and a long farewell.

I might insert dozens of extracts, from various sources, all eulogistic of Sir Hugh Rose and his achievements. I select one only, chiefly on account of its brevity; it will serve as a fair specimen of many others.

He always showed a disposition and determination to fight, whatever odds were against him; in his fights he always punished severely. He marched without cessation from the Nerbudda to the Jumna, following on the heels of the murderer with the certainty and rapidity of the blood-hound; he caught them in their lairs, broke down their fastnesses, and stripped them of their weapons. When confronted by their thousands, he met them with his hundreds, never yielding an inch, and, as at Marathon of old, laid their cohorts in the dust. By day and by night, through the perils and dangers of disease, fatigue, the battlefield, and the burning sun, he led his over-tasked squadrons from victory to victory, never sheathing the awful avenging sword until he had strewn the plains of India with corpses, and scattered the enemy like the four winds.

In the valleys, on the mountains, in the city, on the plains, the whitened bones of mutineers and rebels lie, to tell their tales to all who pass by, and remind them of the avenging march of Sir Hugh Rose's army through Central India.[8]

---

7. Gwalior was in possession of the rebels eighteen days only.

8. See *Generals Rose and Stuart's Indian Campaigns.* To those who would wish for a fuller description of his achievements during that trying campaign, I would recommend the perusal of the above-named book; also *The History of the Indian Mutiny.*

CHAPTER 34

Gwalior Fort

My troop (the K), a battery of artillery, and a part of the 71st were left in charge of the *Phoolbagh* for some time; ourselves and the artillery remaining in tents, pitched on the plain, and the 71st occupying the palace.

While we were there a large body of the Gwalior irregular cavalry, numbering about 2,000 men, were dismounted—that is, their horses were taken away from them. This was effected by the *maharajah* himself in a very masterly manner.

We were all in readiness when His Highness rode in at the head of the cavalry. When he had reached what he thought a suitable place for the purpose, he gave the word for them to retire by files from the right of troops, then turn inwards, dismount, and picket their horses. This being done, he made them fall in by troops at the head of their respective lines, and marched them off at once, minus their horses, to their rage and mortification at being thus easily outwitted, for without their horses they were comparatively useless. They had no help for it and had to go; for the least resistance would have brought us down on them, as we were in waiting for any fracas that might take place.

At midnight there was a regular stampede amongst the horses, a few of them having been cut loose either by the men left in charge of them, or by their owners stealing into the lines and doing so in hopes the loose horses would return to their old lines, and they would thus recover them; or, perhaps, they thought the loose horses would cause ours to break loose as well as their own, and cause great confusion. At any rate, horses were galloping about in all directions; and as the night was intensely dark, it was extremely dangerous. Orders came that we were to hamstring all the loose horses we could; and it was exciting to stand by while a horse dashed past and slash at his hind-legs with our swords, in hopes of cutting the sinews, which would effectually put a stop to his galloping. Several were served this way, and when they were brought up by hamstringing they were put out of their misery as soon as possible.[1]

Meanwhile the sick and wounded of the different detachments were sent up into Gwalior Fort, for the benefit of the cooler atmosphere which was to be obtained on its lofty heights. My troop was shortly afterwards ordered to remove into Morar, where we, with several other troops, were sheltered under some sheds which had been hastily run up for our accommodation.

While staying here, I was sent one day up to Gwalior Fort to bring in the dead body of our hospital sergeant. As he died under peculiar circumstances, I will briefly relate them:—

A sick sergeant of the artillery was in the hospital at the fort, and it seems he was a great friend of Sergeant Culpin, the hospital sergeant. This man always carried a revolver about with him, chiefly from habit. One day the hospital sergeant jokingly reminded him of the uselessness of carrying such a weapon in hospital. The other remarked he might find use for it there as well as anywhere else, and, in a lark, he drew it, exclaiming, "By God, I'll shoot you!" Somehow the weapon went off, and, to the man's horror, shot the unfortunate sergeant, who died within twenty-four hours, leaving a young widow and child to deplore his loss. The artillery sergeant was tried and acquitted with a severe reprimand, as the deed was proved to be done by accident, though the words he had made use of certainly made it look very black against him.

I brought the corpse to Morar, where it was buried. To my great surprise the next day my name was read out in orders as the successor of the sergeant, and the following one saw me installed in Gwalior Fort as acting hospital sergeant. I lived in the fort for some months, and felt the full benefit of the change from the sweltering heat of the plains to the cool and bracing atmosphere of the fort, which, being about 400 feet in height, made the air always deliciously cool and pleasant.

My room looked down on to the city of Gwalior, and it made one

---

1. The cavalry, in India, use entire horses only; and if one breaks loose, it sometimes causes an immense deal of trouble—the others fighting, plunging, and endeavouring to break loose as well. One loose horse at a field-day will often throw a whole troop into confusion; the horses getting into a fearful state of excitement, rearing, plunging, fighting, and using every effort to throw their riders.

feel giddy to look down the perpendicular side of the rock and see the people below. By the aid of a telescope I had a capital opportunity of inspecting the internal economy of many of the establishments near the fort; and I thus witnessed many little domestic episodes, which the performers of never thought were being overlooked by the *Feringee*, or they would have shunned their courtyards and housetops. During my leisure hours I explored all over the place, weaving many a romance in my own mind from a stray couplet or verse of poetry written on the walls of some room in what had probably been the harem—wondering what fair being had written them, and what had been the fate of the writer, and a thousand other extravagances which the lines conjured up, and which only a dreamer could indulge in; and the more I saw of it, the more I was struck with wonder at its vast strength, and the strange freak of nature in erecting this one solid rock in the midst of the plain. I believe no power on earth could ever take it if properly manned and provisioned.

The views from all sides of the fort were magnificent, the country stretching out like a map on all sides, till sky and earth blended together in the distance.

On the side of the fort nearest the *Lushkar*, was a sort of gully or hollow where were some immense idols carved out of the solid rock. Some idea may be formed of the monstrous size of these idols when I state that I have climbed up the steps cut out of the rock at the sides, and have reclined on the under lip of one of them.

In the centre of the fort was a large tank cut out from the solid rock, in which was. a constant supply of clear cold water; the wonder was how water could naturally find its way to such a height.

As the cold season came on, the hospital establishment was shifted from the fort down to Morar again, and was put up in a large building which, I think, had been the hospital for the Gwalior Contingent.

A camel race came off while we were at Morar, and they entered into the spirit of the thing with all the fire of racers, going along at a tremendous swinging pace. There was also an elephant race, and it was something out of the common to see half-a-dozen elephants come thundering along with erect trunks, and shaking the very ground with their ponderous weight.

Among the troops there was a good deal of drill going on—licking a Sikh levy into shape—training the camel corps. This was a new feature in warfare, and likely to be of great service, as after a march or pursuit the infantry can dismount from the camels comparatively fresh. Each camel has a double saddle fitted to its back; on the front saddle sits the native driver, on the rear one sits the infantryman (it should be camelryman). It used to be laughable to see them being drilled. The camels go through their movements with almost as much precision as cavalry, but, till the men got used to it, it was laughable to see how tenaciously they clung to the native driver—for camels are not the easiest animals in the world to ride at a long trot.

Here I used often to receive visits from the chaplain, who had recently arrived from England, and was anxious to gather all the information he could concerning India. I used to have long chats with him, which he evidently enjoyed; and, I need not say, I enlightened him very considerably, to his surprise and horror in many cases.

This gentleman one day, shortly after his arrival, came to me, and said he understood there were several religious men in the regiment, and he wished to know how and where he might be able to see them. I told him if he walked down the horse lines any evening at stable-time he would have an excellent opportunity of doing so, as they would be sure to be there.

"But," inquired the chaplain, looking somewhat mystified, "how can I tell them from the others if I see them?"

"Nothing more simple," I replied; "when you see an awkward, round-shouldered man, or one with weak knees, you may be certain he is one of the parties you are seeking for."

"Do you mean to tell me, then," cried the chaplain, "that religious men are not as smart as other men?"

"Of course they are not," I replied; "look what a shambling spider-legged fellow you had for a clerk last Sunday—he's a specimen."

"Certainly," agreed the chaplain, "*he's* not a very smart man; but they can't *all* be awkward, or, if they are, how do you account for it?"

"I can give no other reason," I replied, looking as serious as I possibly could—for I had great difficulty to keep my countenance—"than that the round shoulders are caused by the weight of sin they bear, and which they jerk up in the way a porter would to ease it, till, like Christian, they may cast it from them; and that constant kneeling makes them give way at the knees."

Another time, the chaplain, who was really a good, kind-hearted man, came to me, as usual, for a chat, and anxious to get some information, he commenced the conversation with—

"Oh, Sergeant, I have just come from the 71st hospital, and I find that they have no less than thirty-four patients suffering from diseases caused by immorality, while in your hospital there are but three; how do you account for that?"

"That is easily accounted for," I replied; "for we keep a stud, and they do not."

"Keep a stud!" exclaimed he, somewhat mystified; "I don't properly understand you."

I then explained to him that so many women were allowed to follow the regiment, and were under its protection, who had a regular tariff, were inspected weekly, and, if necessary, put under medical treatment till well.

"Good heavens!" exclaimed the horror-struck chaplain; "and do you mean to tell me such things are allowed?"

I assured him they were not only allowed, but were considered a great benefit to the men, and a great savings to Government, preventing much sickness, which, but for these regulations, would undoubtedly prevail amongst them.

"But look at the gross immorality!" cried the shocked chaplain, and——"

"Look at the benefit!" I interrupted. "You yourself have just proved the advantage of such a system. The 71st having joined on the road, no women are attached to the regiment, they have thirty-four men sick; we have women attached to the 14th, and we have only three men sick."

This argument was unanswerable; though the chaplain expatiated very strongly on the immorality of the thing, and declared he would do his best, by representing the matter in the proper quarters, to get it put a stop to. I declared that if he did he would be doing an injury to the men which all the good intentions in the world would not justify. That this was an exceptional case of sinning in which "*out of evil cometh good.*" I have never heard whether he succeeded or not, but I think not; in fact, I don't think he ever put in his protest, becoming more reconciled to the system the more he perceived the good derived from it.

Soon after, we were ordered to go by bullock train[2] to Bombay, there to embark for England. Off we started by detachments, one

_____

2. These are carts made to hold two men each, so that they can lie down in them; each cart is drawn by two bullocks. Every few miles distance there is a "bullock station," where the bullocks are changed. This operation does not take a minute to effect, and excepting a halt of two hours or so at midday, for the purpose of getting a meal cooked, the train goes on unceasingly day and night. After travelling about a thousand miles in this manner one's nerves get pretty well shaken up.

troop a day; I bringing up the rear with the hospital establishment,—
not in charge now, however—for, whatever my ability, my services as
a non-commissioned officer were not sufficiently long to entitle me
to the exalted rank of full hospital sergeant, so that when the regiment
got together I was superseded, but was left with my successor for a
month or two to instruct him in his duties.

In due time we reached Bombay, with every nerve in our bodies
vibrating with a month's incessant jolting in the bullock-train. Here
we found the order to proceed to England was countermanded; we
were to return to our old station, Kirkee, where we had the satisfaction of amusing ourselves by breaking in a regiment of young horses,
our own having been left up the country.

Chapter 35

Conclusion

"I thought you said your horse was as quiet as a lamb; why, he 's a perfect brute! I wouldn't have him for any money!" exclaimed the captain, in high dudgeon.

I did not expect he would. This was just what I had anticipated, and what I had carefully paved the way for. After breaking in a horse, and getting him nicely to your hand, it is not pleasant to have him taken away from you, even by your own captain, who has the right of selecting any horse he chooses—and who is generally careful to do so *after* it is broken in.

A magnificent iron-grey had fallen to my share from the remounts; it was admired by everyone, and I was quite proud of my acquisition, and no mother took more pains to teach her little one to run alone than I did to try and train my horse well. From the first moment, however, of my obtaining possession of the horse, I had noticed the longing eye the captain had thrown on it; and I knew that he only waited till the horse was nicely broken in, when he would compliment me by selecting him as his charger—after all the trouble I had taken with him, too.

In anticipation of this, and to cause the captain to wish to get rid of the horse quicker than he took him, I had trained him to kick out lustily if one touched him with the spur when mounting, or on first starting off in a canter. This little arrangement I had, of course, kept entirely to myself.

Sure enough, when the horse was broken in, my forebodings were realised; the captain ordered him to be taken to his bungalow, to make a trial of him. He *did* make a trial of him; got on the horse's back, and was pressing him off into a gentle canter, when the "lamb" gave a bound, throwing up his hind-legs at the same time, and sent the captain flying over his head.

This was devilish strange! so quiet as he always appeared, too. The captain essayed to mount him again; but the horse seemed to object to having him on his back, and unhorsed him again in a twinkling; so that, in sheer disgust, the captain was glad to hand him over to me again, with the reputation of his being a "perfect brute." I thus retained peaceable possession of my charger; but for fear the plot should be suspected, I caused him to let out a kick now and then for the captain's special behoof, who really thought him the "perfect brute" he had described him.

Amusements of all kinds again became the order of the day—or rather night, for our days were devoted to regimental duties—and I spent some very pleasant hours in Kirkee. The 6th Inniskilliugs were quartered in the same barracks with us, and the two regiments were on the best of terms, fraternising on all occasions. The two sergeants' messes were contiguous, and we had many uproarious evenings, the sergeants of both regiments assembling at either mess. In these meetings I always took care to keep myself *compos mentis,* so as to catch every bit of the fun going on.

When a private I was never once in the guard-room, but I had no sooner been made a N. C. O. than I was perpetually getting into some scrape or other, out of which I as constantly succeeded in getting. Most of my scrapes originated from neglect of some trifling detail of duty, or carelessness. When reprimanded by the sergeant-major for some neglect of duty, it was a common habit of mine to pooh-pooh the affair as trifling and immaterial. Indeed, at this time I was generally known by the nickname of "Immaterial." The name originated chiefly in this manner, as well as by making constant use of the word:—

One day the sergeant-major of my troop asked me the number of my horse. I told him I hadn't the remotest idea, but I could easily ascertain. Hereupon, I called the *ghora-wallah,* from whom I quickly obtained the requisite information. The sergeant-major remarked, "You are a queer sort of non-commissioned officer not to know the number of your own horse."

"Sergeant-major," I gravely replied, "It's immaterial what number the horse is. I make it a point to *ride* him as well as I can; not to stare down at his feet to look at his number,"

I cannot here resist relating a joke played by some of our young subs, on a brother officer, who was not much of a favourite either with officers or men, and whom the former looked upon as being snobbish in his ways, and determined to represent as a *bonâ fide* and literal snob;

On a Sunday morning we were marching to church, and as we drew near the bungalow of the snobbish officer in question, those in the rear heard a suppressed titter run through the ranks at the head of the regiment; this titter occasionally fully developed into loud laughter, pursuing its course through the different troops as they successively passed the bungalow. The cause of this laughter was a signboard, on which was usually seen the words Lieut. —— 14th Light Dragoons, informing the passer-by that the individual named on the board resided there, but which on the present occasion had had a few slight additions made, and read as follows:—

Lieutenant ——
(14th Light Dragoons),
Boot and Shoe Maker
Repairs Neatly Executed.
Country Orders promptly attended to.

This had been done by the young officers during the night, and Lieut. ——, had not observed it when leaving his bungalow to go to parade—his back being to it. He must have been rather annoyed at finding himself made a butt of before the whole of the regiment.

Another adventure occurred here at this time of a more serious nature, and led to unpleasant results. The sergeant-major of the officers' mess had recently married a very handsome woman, and had left the service, opening a store in Poona.

A young harum-scarum officer of the regiment must needs fall in love with this woman, and succeeded in inspiring her with the same sentiment, and it ended in her proving unfaithful to her husband; the two carrying on an illicit intercourse unsuspected for some time—the young officer visiting the frail one in the disguise of a lady, which his youthful appearance enabled him to do admirably.

The husband at last got scent of these stolen meetings, and one day caught the guilty pair together; but the officer dashed through an open window, mounted a horse, and galloped off to his bungalow at Kirkee, followed shortly after by the injured husband bent on having satisfaction for the injury.

On arriving at the bungalow, the husband walked straight into the room where the gay Lothario was, and pulling out a pistol and pointing it at him, exclaimed, "B——, I've come to shoot you!" Suiting the action to the word, he fired, and shot the officer through the body. The husband was tried, and got twelve months' imprisonment. The young officer was so dangerously wounded that his life was despaired of for some time; and we had to leave him in India when we left, it not being safe to move him. He, however, eventually recovered, and rejoined us in Ireland, apparently not much the worse for the wound.

At length, after having been in India nineteen years, the regiment again proceeded to Bombay; and this time embarked for home, there being only twelve of the men who originally came out with the regiment to return with it. After a pleasant voyage we reached Falmouth, where, much to our chagrin—the regiment consisting almost entirely of Englishmen—we received orders to proceed to Ireland.

This arrangement gave great [dissatisfaction to everyone, and lost the country the services of over 300 good men, whose term of service had already expired, or would soon do so, and who, but for this, would have taken on for another term; the men invariably, as soon as their time was up, leaving the service, their places being recruited by dumpties, so that in a few months the regiment was not recognisable.

My sabretasche is not half empty yet, I find it still contains a large number of scraps.

Shall I go on? Shall I relate my adventures in Ireland, in England, in China, where I now am, and. where I have been fifteen years? How I woke up one morning and found myself, after a good deal of knocking about, located in the heart of Peking—of all places in the world—close under the walls of the Imperial Palace? Shall I? Reader, it rests entirely with you whether I conclude my adventures with this volume, or whether, having your approval in this, I am emboldened to produce a second by making another collection of *Scraps from my Sabretasche.*

www.ingramcontent.com/pod-product-compliance
Lightning Source LLC
Chambersburg PA
CBHW021100090426
42738CB00006B/437